FOOTSTEPS EVERY DAY

Mark
A Devotional Commentary

BOB ROGNLIEN

FOOTSTEPS EVERY DAY, Volume Two
Mark: A Devotional Commentary
Copyright © Bob Rognlien 2023

All rights reserved. No part of this book may be reproduced without written permission, except
for brief quotations in books and reviews. For information contact GX Books, bobrognlien@gmail.com or www.bobrognlien.com.

All Scripture quotations are from the Christian Standard Bible® (CSB®), Copyright © 2017 by Holman Bible Publishers. Used by permission. Christian Standard Bible® and CSB® are federally registered trademarks of Holman Bible Publishers.

Cover Design: Timothy J. Bergren
Book Design: Amit Dey
Editor: Robert Neely
ISBN: 978-0-9815247-8-8
Published by GX Books

DEDICATION

To my daughters-in-law, Amy and Taylor.
You are truly the daughters we never had,
the wives we prayed our sons would find,
and the mothers of the most amazing grandchildren ever.
We are so grateful for you!

ACKNOWLEDGEMENTS

I want to express my gratitude to all those who supported me, prayed for me, and made the writing of this book and series possible. Specifically, I want to thank Pam Rognlien, Chris Pudel, Heidi Hollings for carefully rooting out my many mistakes. Any which remain are mine alone. Thanks to Robert Neely for editing the manuscript and Amit Dey for designing the interior pages. They have both made the book eminently more readable. Special thanks to Tim Bergren for designing another great book cover. Above all I give thanks to Jesus, the Great Shepherd of the Sheep, who continues inviting us all to listen to his voice and follow him by taking steps of faith every day. Come join us on the adventure!

INTRODUCTION

In the first chapter of this Gospel, Mark describes Jesus' predictable pattern of spending time alone with his heavenly Father the King. *Very early in the morning, while it was still dark, he got up, went out, and made his way to a deserted place; and there he was praying.* (Mark 1:35)

Those who follow Jesus recognize this is a critical rhythm of discipleship—seeking to become more like him by hearing and responding to what he is saying every day. Paul says, *"So faith comes from what is heard, and what is heard comes through the message about Christ."* (Romans 10:17) When we listen for the voice of Jesus speaking through his written Word, the Holy Spirit plants faith in our hearts. When we exercise that faith by taking a concrete step in the footsteps of Jesus, we grow as his fruitful disciples and learn to live a more Jesus-shaped life.

Footsteps Every Day is a series of devotional commentaries on the New Testament, designed to help followers of Jesus establish a regular pattern of spending time alone with God, reading Scripture, listening in prayer, and responding with a step of faith. Volume Two, *Mark,* is the second in the series and offers brief reflections on 64 passages that make up Mark's account of Jesus' life, drawing on history, archaeology, and culture to illuminate the Way of Jesus and help you follow him with concrete steps of faith.

Each of these devotional commentaries can be read on its own at your own pace, or you can read all four Gospels in succession. If you read six passages a week, the first four volumes will take you on an incredible year-long journey through the Gospels, following the life of Jesus and reflecting on every recorded thing he said and did during his life on earth!

These books can also be used as biblical commentaries by looking up a specific passage you are studying to gain fresh insights from the historical and cultural background to inform you as you teach others and apply God's Word to daily life.

Here are my recommendations for a fruitful devotional journey in Jesus' *Footsteps Every Day*:

- Pick a time in which you have the highest likelihood of being consistent each day. Set aside at least 15 minutes, or better 30 minutes.
- Pick a place where you will be the least distracted and interrupted. Make yourself comfortable but adopt an attentive posture. Get too comfortable and you will fall asleep!
- Read the Scripture passage in your own Bible. My writing is based on the text from the Christian Standard Bible, an excellent and often overlooked translation, but you can use any version you find helpful. Read it again.
- Take some time to prayerfully listen as you scan over the passage, noting what God seems to be pointing out to you.
- Highlight important phrases and make relevant notes in the margins. (Even digital Bibles allow for this. I use the [Olive Tree App](#).)
- Read the commentary provided in *Footsteps Every Day*.
- Prayerfully ask God what he is saying to you through all the above. Listen and write down what is coming to you in the space provided (or type it as a digital note if you are reading the eBook edition).
- Then ask God to show you the next step of faith he wants you to take.
- Write down your step of faith in the space provided (or type it as a digital note if you are reading the eBook edition).
- Take that step of faith!
- If you are having trouble taking that step, share it with someone you trust and ask them to pray for you to exercise the faith God is giving you. Take that step of faith!
- Rinse and repeat!

- At the end of every six days, there is a section called "Footsteps Every Week." Use this space to reflect on the readings from the past week, summarize your insights from each day, identify any major themes, consider any new predictable patterns God is calling you to establish, and identify the most significant verse to memorize.

When we read God's Word and listen to what Jesus is saying to us through the Spirit, it produces faith in our hearts. Our role is to respond to what Jesus is saying by exercising that faith, taking the next step in following the footsteps of Jesus. We are not trying to change ourselves by moral willpower, but rather are putting ourselves in the place where God's Spirit can transform us from the inside out and produce through us good fruit that lasts. This is what it means to live as a Jesus-shaped disciple. Please don't approach this as a religious task that you must perform but receive this opportunity as a gracious invitation to draw near to Jesus, hear his voice, and follow where he leads you on this great adventure of discipleship!

DAY 1

READ AND LISTEN: MARK 1:1-8

Take a minute to listen for what the Spirit is saying in these verses…

COMMENT AND CONSIDER

In the first century, a wealthy Jewish merchant family from Cyprus owned a spacious home on the southwest hill of Jerusalem. They came from a priestly background, and two members of the family became followers of Jesus—a man named Joseph, nicknamed Barnabas ("Son of Encouragement"), and his cousin Mary, the mother of a boy named John Mark. The night before he was arrested, Jesus arranged with Mary to use the upper room of their home in Jerusalem to share the Passover meal with his disciples. After Jesus' death and resurrection, this home seems to have become the base of operations for the leaders of Jesus' movement in Jerusalem. It is where a number of significant events took place in the years to come, including the outpouring of the Holy Spirit on Pentecost.

When Barnabas and Saul were commissioned by the leaders of the church in Antioch to set out on the first missionary journey, Barnabas invited his young nephew John Mark to accompany them. Although John Mark didn't complete the journey, this experience, along with all the things he must have witnessed in the family home back in Jerusalem, had a significant impact on him. According to tradition, he eventually ended up as a disciple of the Apostle Peter in Rome and took notes while listening as Peter told his eyewitness accounts of what Jesus said and did during his life on earth. This became the basis for the Gospel of Mark. Mark wrote in a time of great turmoil, when a series of unstable Emperors ruled in Rome, and the First Jewish Revolt wrought havoc in Palestine. Mark's Gospel offers an account of Jesus' life that is profoundly good news for people facing pressure and uncertainty.

In his opening line, Mark announces Jesus is the Messiah, also called the Son of God. It is incredibly Good News when Jesus is King, in sharp contrast to the violent and unstable emperors and kings who were making their lives so difficult. Then Mark introduces us to John the Baptist and his mission of preparation. John was out in the Jordan Valley dressed like the great prophet Elijah who was prophesied to return before the Messiah appeared. (See Malachi 4:5-6.) Mark quotes John's mission statement from Isaiah 40:3, *"Prepare the way for the Lord; make his paths straight!"*

John prepared the way for the coming of the Messiah by inviting people to join him in the desert wilderness and immerse themselves in the waters of the Jordan River. First-century Jews were used to immersing themselves in ritual baths (Hebrew: *mikveh*) for the symbolic cleansing of external ritual impurity. John's baptism of repentance was something much deeper. This baptism was for repentance and the forgiveness of sins. The word "repent" (Greek: *metanoia*) literally means to have a changed mind. John was preparing people for the coming Messiah by inviting them to receive a whole new perspective from God, as well as a brand-new start. It was about undergoing an internal recalibration in which God reoriented their lives so they would be ready when the Messiah appeared. John told them the coming Messiah would immerse them in the very presence and power of God.

Are you ready for what Jesus wants to do in your life? Are there internal roadblocks keeping the Holy Spirit from working in you? Are you going through the external motions, or are you ready to let Jesus do a deep work of repentance and forgiveness in your life?

Reflect and Respond

What is Jesus saying to me right now?

What step of faith is Jesus calling me to take today?

DAY 2

READ AND LISTEN: MARK 1:9-13
Take a minute to listen for what the Spirit is saying in these verses…

COMMENT AND CONSIDER

Jesus chose to begin his mission by going to John in the desert and submitting to baptism. This seems a strange way to launch a messianic career! Why not go to the Temple in Jerusalem and impress the crowds with some miracles? Because Jesus was not setting out to impress anyone or draw a crowd. Nor was he coming to prepare himself through confession and repentance. John's baptism of preparation was coming to an end. Jesus was doing something new.

Jesus inaugurated the New Covenant promised by God through Jeremiah, *"I will put my teaching within them and write it on their hearts. I will be their God, and they will be my people. No longer will one teach his neighbor or his brother, saying, 'Know the Lord,' for they will all know me, from the least to the greatest of them"—this is the Lord's declaration. "For I will forgive their iniquity and never again remember their sin."* (Jeremiah 31:33-34) This New Covenant is not based on the Law carved into tablets of stone. This is a covenant of mercy and grace written on the hearts of God's people!

The place where John baptized was at the Jordan River in the southern part of Israel, just to the east of the ancient city of Jericho. Tradition tells us this was the same place where Joshua led the people of Israel across the river into the Promised Land. This spot had been off limits to visitors for over forty years due to regional conflicts, but now we can visit this idyllic location on the Jordan River. Each time we visit, we invite people to renew their baptism by being immersed in the very same spot John baptized Jesus. It is truly a powerful experience!

When Jesus came up out of the water that day, the sky was torn open. The Holy Spirit descended upon Jesus, like the many white doves we still see today at the site of Jesus' baptism. A voice from heaven declared, *"You are my beloved Son; with you I am well-pleased."* The Father was announcing Jesus' true identity. The Father was expressing his love and favor over his Son! The New Covenant is an invitation into a relationship of love and grace with the Father. It is an invitation to discover who you really are, a beloved child of God!

From this powerful experience of love and grace, the Spirit *"drove"* Jesus into the harsh desert wilderness just to the east of the river. Jesus entered an extended time of fasting, the spiritual discipline that teaches us to depend on God and seek him above all else. Here the devil began to attack Jesus. Mark doesn't give us any details of this epic wrestling match, but we know that Jesus prevailed, and he came out of the desert stronger than when he went in.

Do you know who you really are? On what is your identity based? Is it what you own or what you have accomplished? Jesus shows us where to find our true identity. It is in the waters of baptism. The Father is the only one who can tell you who you really are. You are his beloved child. Not because of anything you have done, but because that is who he has made you. This is the New Covenant of grace in Jesus. This is how we face and overcome the inevitable battles that lie ahead. Jesus is showing us it all begins with knowing who we really are. Who are you?

Reflect and Respond

What is Jesus saying to me right now?

What step of faith is Jesus calling me to take today?

DAY 3

READ AND LISTEN: MARK 1:14-20

Take a minute to listen for what the Spirit is saying in these verses...

COMMENT AND CONSIDER

The four eyewitness accounts of Jesus' life, death, and resurrection recorded in the Bible are called "Gospels." Gospel means "good news." When Jesus finished his time of testing in the desert wilderness, he returned north to his home region of Galilee and began telling people good news. He told them that a special moment in time had finally come. The Greek word for linear time is *chronos*, which is time that simply ticks along from one second to the next. But Mark uses the Greek word *kairos* to express this special moment in time Jesus was announcing. Rather than a linear unfolding of time, *kairos* is like coming to a crossroads in time. It is that moment when something new is happening and we have to make a decision. Will we continue on straight ahead, or will we turn right or left?

Jesus said, *"The time [kairos] is fulfilled, and the kingdom of God has come near."* This is the Good News! All the suffering, pain, and injustice of this world is a result of humanity rejecting God as our rightful King. When Adam and Eve decided to rule their own lives, God's perfect creation was profoundly broken, and so were they. Ever since we have toiled by the sweat of our brow, bringing forth thorns and thistles. Ever since we have borne pain and conflict as we try to rule over each other. (See Genesis 3:1-19.) This is the bad news with which we are all painfully familiar.

God is all good. God is all powerful. God is all knowing. God is all present. When God is King, things are good, because he is righteous, holy, and just. Above all God is love, and it is for love that we are created. When God is King, love prevails. When love prevails, there is peace and joy, fulfillment and fruitfulness. This is what Jesus meant when he declared the Good News of the Kingdom of God. God is going to be our King once again!

Jesus explained this new reign of God has not yet been fully enacted but is in the process of coming. The phrase *"at hand"* translates the Greek word *engidzo*, which describes something that has begun to arrive but has not fully come yet. It is like a moving train entering the station. It is here, but it has not yet fully arrived. Jesus said the Good News is that the restored reign of God as King over his creation is now in the process of arriving. The Kingdom of God is coming!

Jesus goes on to explain that there are two primary ways for us to respond to this Good News of the Kingdom, *"Repent and believe the good news!"* *"Repent"* means to get a new mind and *"believe"* means putting faith into action. Listening to God is how we get a new mind. We ask Jesus, "what are you saying to me?" Paul tells us faith comes from hearing Jesus' personal word to us. (See Romans 10:17.) Once we have repented by listening for the word of faith, then we respond to what God is saying by exercising that faith. This is what it means to believe. We ask Jesus, "what is the next step of faith you are calling me to take?"

This is what it means to be a disciple. Disciples listen to the voice of Jesus and exercise faith by following in his footsteps. When Jesus met the four fishermen, Simon, Andrew, James, and John, he shared this Good News of the Kingdom with them. They allowed that word of Jesus to change their minds and plant faith in their heart. They exercised that faith by putting down their nets and beginning to follow in the footsteps of Jesus. They were going to learn a whole new kind of fishing with God as their King! How are you responding to the Good News of the Kingdom?

Reflect and Respond
What is Jesus saying to me right now?

What step of faith is Jesus calling me to take today?

DAY 4

READ AND LISTEN: MARK 1:21-34

Take a minute to listen for what the Spirit is saying in these verses...

COMMENT AND CONSIDER

When Jesus spoke, people listened in a different way than they did to other teachers. Most scribes quoted the teaching of other rabbis to make their points. They told people things that other people had told them about God. Jesus was different. He spoke directly as a representative of God. That was because he knew who he was. God was his Father, and he was God's Son. He spoke and acted out of that relationship. As he said, *"So the things that I speak, I speak just as the Father has told me."* (John 12:50) This is what it means to say Jesus spoke with authority. He did not speak on behalf of himself, but as a representative of his Father the King. That is why his words impacted people so powerfully. As Mark records, *"They were astonished at his teaching because he was teaching them as one who had authority, and not like the scribes."*

But it wasn't just Jesus' words that carried the authority of his Father the King; it was also his actions. Jesus said, *"Truly I tell you, the Son is not able to do anything on his own, but only what he sees the Father doing. For whatever the Father does, the Son likewise does these things."* (John 5:19) The reason Jesus could heal people of their diseases and deliver demonized people from their oppression was not that he was God. He was divine, but he set that aside when he became fully human and operated out of his humanity for the three decades he walked this earth. (See Philippians 2:6-7.)

When Jesus saw the Father wanted to heal, he exercised faith in the authority given to him as a son of the King and through the power of the Holy Spirit healed people. In this case, in the synagogue of Capernaum, Jesus saw that his Father wanted to deliver this man from these unclean spirits, so he spoke as an authorized representative of the King, acted in faith, and the unclean spirits came out! Jesus was doing something we can learn to do as well. Jesus' brother James explains it this way, *"Therefore, submit to God. Resist the devil, and he will flee from you."* (James 4:7)

Capernaum was a medium-sized fishing town on the north shore of the Sea of Galilee. It was where the four fishermen Simon, Andrew, James, and John lived with their extended families. Capernaum has been extensively excavated, and archaeologists have discovered the remains of the first-century synagogue where Jesus taught as well as the home of Simon and Andrew's extended family. In biblical times multiple nuclear families typically lived together in the same compound, sharing life together and carrying out a family business. Simon and Andrew's extended family owned a beautiful home right next to the waterfront where they carried out their family fishing business. It was into this very home that Simon invited Jesus after the synagogue service was over.

It was a great honor for their family to host a rabbi in their home, and Jesus further blessed them by healing Simon's mother-in-law. She promptly served them a nice Sabbath meal. Everyone would have been thrilled. But then Jesus did something radical and unexpected. He opened the outer door of their extended family home and invited everyone in town to join them! Pretty soon the whole courtyard was filled with people. This was not the way things worked. You didn't invite just anyone into your home—only those who would bring honor to the family. Since Jesus invited the sick and the demon-possessed, it was obvious everyone was invited. There, in that home, he began to heal and deliver them.

Jesus showed them you don't have to go to the synagogue to experience God's presence and power. Your own home and family are the place where the Kingdom of God is meant to be lived out. Where do you experience God most powerfully? How can you bring that into your home and family?

REFLECT AND RESPOND

What is Jesus saying to me right now?

What step of faith is Jesus calling me to take today?

DAY 5

READ AND LISTEN: MARK 1:35-45

Take a minute to listen for what the Spirit is saying in these verses…

COMMENT AND CONSIDER

Being a disciple is learning to know what the rabbi knows, as well as learning to do what the rabbi does. The goal is to become like the rabbi. When Jesus said, *"Follow me,"* he invited men and women to come close enough to him so they could hear his words and observe his actions. His words were a source of incredible information, but his actions were an example that called for imitation. Jesus said, *"I am the way, the truth, and the life."* (John 14:6) Jesus called people to believe in his Truth but also to follow his Way. Many of us have focused on studying the truth of Jesus' teachings, but often we forget to imitate the patterns and rhythms of the way he lived. Perhaps that is why our lives often don't look much like his amazing life.

The secret of Jesus' authority and power was the incredibly close relationship he had with his Father the King. Jesus had intentional rhythms in his life that nurtured that intimate connection with the Father. As we see in this passage, Jesus rose early each morning while it was still dark and went to a *"deserted place"* so he could have some quality time alone with his Father. The hillsides above Capernaum are strewn with volcanic basalt stones which makes it difficult to plant crops there. This is probably the deserted place where Jesus went to watch the sun rise over the beautiful Sea of Galilee each morning while spending time in prayer.

At the end of his ministry, Jesus gave the disciples a picture of what it means for us to develop this kind of relationship with him. *"I am the vine; you are the branches. The one who remains in me and I in him produces much fruit, because you can do nothing without me."* (John 15:5) The Greek word *meno* is translated *"remain"* here. It means to dwell or abide in the same place. There is a rhythm of abiding and a rhythm of fruit-bearing. Jesus intentionally spent time dwelling in the presence of his Father, and this was why he was able to do all the incredibly fruitful things he did.

Jesus' time alone with the Father was not the only daily rhythm in his life. He also had a regular rhythm of telling people about God's Kingdom and demonstrating the power of God's loving reign. When the disciples came frantically looking for him that morning, Jesus didn't send them away as if he had become a reclusive monk. Instead, he stepped out of his time of abiding with the Father and into all the things his Father was calling him to do that day.

He told people the Good News of the Kingdom. He demonstrated the nature of that Kingdom by casting out demons. He touched an untouchable leper and made him clean so he could rejoin his family. That is how the Kingdom of God works. No one is an outcast. Everyone is welcome. This is the good Kingdom fruit that came from Jesus' intentional rhythm of abiding with his Father the King.

Are you intentionally following the Way of Jesus in addition to studying his Truth? What daily rhythms help you stay closely connected to the Father, Son, and Holy Spirit? Is there a new rhythm Jesus might be inviting you to add to this time of daily Scripture reading? What good fruit do you think Jesus wants to help you bear out of your deepening connection with him?

REFLECT AND RESPOND
What is Jesus saying to me right now?

What step of faith is Jesus calling me to take today?

DAY 6

READ AND LISTEN: MARK 2:1-12

Take a minute to listen for what the Spirit is saying in these verses...

COMMENT AND CONSIDER

One of Jesus' regular rhythms was going out on mission trips with his full-time disciples, ministering to the many towns and villages of Galilee, but then returning to the extended family home of Simon and Andrew in Capernaum. The Greek word for an extended family and the home in which they shared life together is *oikos*. This word can be translated *"household," "house,"* or *"family."* An *oikos* was made up of multiple generations of relatives and friends who all contributed to a common family business. In the first century, everyone who could lived as part of an *oikos*, because it was the best way to protect and provide for the ones you loved.

An *oikos* house was typically comprised of multiple rooms built around a central courtyard. The house had strong outer walls with no windows, almost like a small fortress. All the doors and windows of the rooms opened inward to the courtyard. A strong outer door led into the courtyard which gave access to all the rooms of the house. Usually, a set of steps just inside the outer door led up to a flat rooftop where they would dry fish and fruit, and even sleep at night during the warm summer months.

It is significant that, already at the beginning of chapter two, Mark refers to Simon and Andrew's *oikos* as Jesus' *"home."* He was no longer a visitor there; he had become part of the extended family. But the family was changing. No longer did they hide behind the walls of their family compound, only allowing in people "like us." Now they opened the outer door and invited everyone in. Often the courtyard was so filled with people that there was no more room and people overflowed out the door.

This is the setting when four friends heard Jesus was *"at home"* (literally "in the *oikos*"), and thus tried to bring their paralyzed friend to him for healing. When they arrived, they discovered the courtyard was so packed with people that they couldn't get to Jesus. However, they could access the steps inside the outer door. So they carried their friend up onto the flat roof above the room where Jesus was teaching. The roofs were made of layers of mud and straw laid over rafters. Each fall they had to be resealed with a new layer of mud and straw, rolled flat with a heavy stone roller.

These four friends began to dig through the mud-thatched roof above Jesus' head, making a large opening and a huge mess! They lowered their paralyzed friend through the roof to Jesus, who didn't see the mess as much as their faith. Although Jesus saw this man's obvious physical ailment, he also saw a deeper spiritual paralysis and so said to him, *"Son, your sins are forgiven."* This immediately upset the religious teachers because they believed only God had the authority to forgive sins. Jesus was aware of their objections, so he pointed out that if he had the authority to heal, he must also have the authority to forgive. Then he called the man to his feet, and the man stood up, picked up his mat, and walked in front of them all!

What are you willing to do to bring those you love closer to Jesus? What are the paralyzed places in your life where you need Jesus' forgiveness and healing? Often the obvious ailments in our lives are not the ones that are holding us back most. Sometimes we need to dig deeper to find out what is really going on. Are you willing to dig deeper and make a mess?

Reflect and Respond

What is Jesus saying to me right now?

What step of faith is Jesus calling me to take today?

Footsteps Every Week: Review

Write a brief summary of what Jesus said to you each day this past week and the step of faith he called you to take:

Monday

Tuesday

Wednesday

Thursday

Friday

Saturday

Footsteps Every Week: Reflect

Big Picture
As you look over what Jesus has said to you this past week, do you see any themes? What is the most important thing you need to remember and believe?

Predictable Pattern
As you look over what Jesus called you to do this past week, is there a new predictable pattern he is inviting you to establish in your life with God and others?

Plant the Word
As you look over the readings from this past week, write out the passage that feels most important for you and memorize it over the next week:

DAY 7

READ AND LISTEN: MARK 2:13-17

Take a minute to listen for what the Spirit is saying in these verses…

COMMENT AND CONSIDER

The Roman Empire controlled most the Mediterranean world at the time of Jesus. The Imperial strategy was to invade and conquer neighboring regions, subjugate the people but keep them productive, tax them as heavily as possible, and send the collected goods and money back to Rome. In 63 BC the Roman General Pompey conquered Jerusalem, and Rome took control of the land of Israel. In 40 BC the Romans appointed Herod the Great to rule Judea on their behalf, which he did with an iron fist and a lavish lifestyle. To keep Rome happy and support the Herodian's spending habits, even the poorest peasants were forced to pay about 50% of their income in taxes plus rent on their land. It was a crushing financial burden for most people.

To collect these taxes, the Herodians employed industrious members of the local population who could extract the required payments and who were allowed to keep any additional funds they could extort as their own salary. Understandably, these Jewish tax collectors were the most hated people in their community, considered political traitors and religiously unclean. The rabbis even taught it was allowable to lie to a tax collector because they were so corrupt!

Just east of Capernaum lay the border between Galilee, ruled by Herod Antipas, and Gaulantis, ruled by his half-brother Herod Philip. Antipas had established a tax booth to collect tolls from the merchants who shipped their goods from Philip's territory into his. Levi, whose Roman name was Matthew, was the tax collector who ran that booth. He would have heard about the incredible things Jesus was saying and doing around Capernaum. Maybe he had drawn near to the edge of the crowds that gathered around Jesus to hear his teaching and witness his miracles.

We don't know what put Levi on Jesus' radar, but when Jesus approached the tax collection booth and invited Levi to follow him, it was one of the most shocking things Jesus ever did! The rest of the disciples' heads must have been spinning. How could Jesus call a traitor like Levi into his inner circle of disciples? How could they share meals with this unclean sinner?

It is important to note that Jesus not only invited Levi into his spiritual family, but also accepted Levi's invitation to a banquet in his *oikos* with his fellow tax collectors and his openly sinful friends. The Pharisees (literally "the separated ones") were a sect of the scribes who obsessed over meticulously observing the countless rules of ritual purity the rabbis had developed. They were especially concerned about what food they ate, what dishes they used, and with whom they shared a table. Anyone who didn't display the same zeal for following all the ceremonial and symbolic rules was strictly excluded from any meal in which they participated.

Even entering the home of a tax collector was completely out of bounds for a religious Jew, so when the Pharisees heard Jesus and his disciples were sharing a meal at Levi's house with all his unclean and sinful friends, they were outraged. Jesus responded to their criticism with the profound statement, *"It is not those who are well who need a doctor, but those who are sick. I didn't come to call the righteous, but sinners."* By sharing meals with those considered unclean and sinful by the religious community, Jesus powerfully demonstrated the radical acceptance and free grace of the Kingdom of God. It is no wonder so many from outside the religious establishment were moved by Jesus and followed him.

Who do you know who is considered unclean and openly sinful? What is your posture toward them? What would it look like to demonstrate to them the radical grace and inclusion of God's Kingdom?

Reflect and Respond

What is Jesus saying to me right now?

What step of faith is Jesus calling me to take today?

DAY 8

READ AND LISTEN: MARK 2:18-22

Take a minute to listen for what the Spirit is saying in these verses...

COMMENT AND CONSIDER

The biblical practice of fasting is abstaining from food for a period as an act of mourning, humility, repentance, and to become more aware of our dependence on God. The only biblically prescribed fast for the people of Israel is once a year on the Day of Atonement when they were to *"practice self-denial,"* traditionally interpreted as fasting from food, drink, sex, and bathing. (See Leviticus 16:29-30.) There were seasons in the life of the people of Israel when special fasts were called to help the people turn back to God, but no other fast days mandated in the Bible. John the Baptist and his disciples were known for their ascetic practices which included regular fasting.

Jesus told a parable about an especially self-righteous man who considered himself better than others because, he said among other things, *"I fast twice a week."* (Luke 18:12) He may have been reflecting the practice of the Pharisees who, according to some sources, fasted on Mondays and Thursdays. Although Jesus began his public ministry with an epic 40-day fast in the desert wilderness, he and his disciples did not have a regular rhythm of fasting. The Pharisees, who focused on public religious rituals as a kind of scorecard of holiness, continued their criticism of Jesus for not being strict enough in his piety according to their measures.

Jesus was not rejecting fasting per se but was saying there are seasons when fasting is appropriate and seasons when it does not apply. In the Hebrew Scriptures, God is often portrayed as a bridegroom, an image Jesus applies to himself. (See Isaiah 62:4-5 for example.) He reminded them no one would fast during a wedding feast. It would be an insult to the hospitality of the host family. Since Jesus the bridegroom was present, it was not a season for fasting. In Mark's first allusion to his death, Jesus said the day was coming when his followers would mourn and fasting would be appropriate.

This is another example in a long line of instances where Jesus was true to the written Scriptures but was not bound to human traditions and religious rituals. To illustrate how the coming Kingdom of God challenges old human traditions, Jesus offered two images from everyday life. Everyone knew not to sew a patch of new cloth on an old garment because it would shrink when washed in hot water and thus tear away from the stiches. New wine expands as it ferments and stretched out the leather wineskins which were used to store it. Everyone knew not to put new wine into old, stretched-out wineskins, because the new wine would stretch it further until it burst.

Jesus' point is that the Kingdom of God challenges our old assumptions about what constitutes a truly good life. Old assumptions can't adequately contain the new revelation we have in Jesus. For that reason, Jesus developed new teachings, patterns, and rhythms for his followers so they could learn to live in a new way under God's righteous rule. That is what he meant when he said, *"I am the way, the truth, and the life."* (John 14:6) The Kingdom is coming, Jesus is the King, and he is showing us how to participate in that new reality.

What are some of the old religious rules or assumptions you grew up with that may not apply or be helpful in the Kingdom of God? What are some new wineskins you need in order to carry Jesus' new wine to those around you?

Reflect and Respond

What is Jesus saying to me right now?

What step of faith is Jesus calling me to take today?

DAY 9

READ AND LISTEN: MARK 2:23-3:6
Take a minute to listen for what the Spirit is saying in these verses...

COMMENT AND CONSIDER
When God created the Universe and appointed the man and woman as the overseers of creation, he commanded them to take a full day of rest on the seventh day before engaging in their work, from sundown on Friday until sundown on Saturday. This was a unique practice in the ancient world and one of the key markers that distinguished the people of Israel from the surrounding pagan nations. Those who broke the Sabbath were considered guilty of defiling the Covenant and making Israel liable to the wrath of God. By the time of Jesus, the rabbis had added many layers of interpretation to the simple Sabbath command. These rules included detailed regulations about what could be carried, what you could touch, and how far you could walk.

Jesus did not place much value on the rabbinical interpretations passed down by oral tradition. He was committed to fulfilling the intent of the Law, not the letter. The Law allowed snacking on your neighbors' crops while they were still in the field as long as you didn't actually harvest them with tools and containers. (See Deuteronomy 23:24-25.) Farm fields were outside the village and had no fences, only marker stones. For this reason, walking paths often wound through farmer's fields. This is the hardened ground of the "*path*" on which some seed falls in Jesus' parable of the soils. (See Matthew 13:4.)

One Sabbath day Jesus' disciples were walking on a path that wound through a field of grain. Since they were hungry, they casually plucked heads of grain, rubbed them between their hands, and ate the raw kernels that fell out of the husks. The Pharisees criticized them for violating their rules against harvesting grain on the Sabbath, because by loosening the kernels from their husks they were technically harvesting the grain. Jesus reminded them of a time David set aside ceremonial food regulations on the Sabbath for the sake of human need.

When God established the Tabernacle, he commanded the priests to put out twelve loaves of bread each Sabbath as an offering to God. Only the priests were allowed to eat this "showbread." (See Leviticus 24:5-9.) When David arrived in Nob and needed food, the priest gave David the consecrated bread to eat. (See 1 Samuel 21:1-6.) Jesus explained his point by saying, *"The Sabbath was made for man and not man for the Sabbath."* The day of rest was meant to be a gift that brings blessing and life to people, not a burden that depletes and exhausts people.

Mark immediately pivots to a man with a withered hand in the synagogue on the Sabbath. The rabbis conceded that lifesaving work on the Sabbath was allowed, but not anything that could wait until the next day. They watched Jesus to see what he would do, so Jesus asked, *"Is it lawful to do good on the Sabbath or to do evil, to save life or to kill?"* He showed how the religious teachers had taken something that was good, the gift of restorative rest, and turned it into something evil with burdensome regulations that stand in the way of doing God's will. To illustrate his point, he called the man forward and healed his hand. He did good not evil! Jesus demonstrated the true purpose of Sabbath and his own authority as interpreter of God's Word. Already the Pharisees began to plot with their political enemies, the Herodians, how they could have Jesus killed.

Do you enjoy the gift of 24-hours of rest each week which God is offering you? If not, why? How can you honor and receive the precious gift of Sabbath without turning it into a burdensome rule?

Reflect and Respond

What is Jesus saying to me right now?

What step of faith is Jesus calling me to take today?

DAY 10

READ AND LISTEN: MARK 3:7-19
Take a minute to listen for what the Spirit is saying in these verses…

COMMENT AND CONSIDER
Already Jesus' popularity and fame was building to a fever pitch. Word of his powerful teaching and supernatural healings had spread beyond the Jewish towns of Galilee and drew crowds of people from across Israel, the Gentile regions east of the Jordan River, and as far away as the Mediterranean coast north of Israel. Jesus was overwhelmed by the crush of crowds pressing in to hear and touch him. Just west of Capernaum, on the northern shore of the Sea of Galilee, is a small inlet formed by a semi-circular hillside sloping up from the lake called "Sower's Cove." It seems to be the place where Jesus taught the crowds from Simon's boat so he wouldn't be crushed by them.

After the crowds dispersed, Jesus went up on the hillside overlooking the lake and called together his wider group of disciples. These men and women had been gathering in the house of Simon and Andrew, listening to Jesus' teaching, observing his way of life, and experiencing the transforming power of God. These people had answered Jesus' call to follow him, but still lived in their own homes and worked in their own family businesses. Luke refers to this wider group as the 72 whom Jesus sent out on mission. (See Luke 10:1.)

But now Jesus decided to publicly call 12 of them to leave their jobs to live and travel with him full-time. The decision to choose twelve men recalls the twelve tribes of Israel, and it represented Jesus' mission to call the Jewish people back to their original identity as the family of God and their mission to be a light to the nations. In addition, three of these twelve disciples formed an inner circle, who Jesus sometimes called to himself for extraordinary moments. These disciples are named first in Mark's list: Simon, James, and John. Sometimes Andrew, named fourth in the list, was included in this group as well.

A relatively small pool of Jewish names was used in first-century Palestine, so people often shared a name such as Mary, Simon, or Judah. For this reason, it was common to add a second name as an identifier, such as the name of a father or a hometown. Jesus seemed to enjoy giving his disciples colorful nicknames, such as Simon "the Rock," and James and John, "the Sons of Thunder." The other Simon is described as "the Zealot," which could mean he used to be radically committed to following all the purity laws and religious rituals of the rabbinical traditions. (See Paul's self-description in Galatians 1:14.) Or it could mean he was formerly a member of the Jewish nationalist group called The Zealots whose headquarters in the fortified city of Gamla was not far from Capernaum.

Here we are reminded that discipleship is a relationship. First of all, it is about getting to know Jesus personally and learning to follow him. Secondly, it is about getting to know others who are ahead of us on the journey and imitating the aspects of their lives that look like Jesus. Paul invited the Corinthians to *"Imitate me, as I also imitate Christ."* (1 Corinthians 11:1) This is the posture of a mature disciple. As disciples of Jesus, we are to invite others into our lives who we can help learn how to follow him. This is what it means to make disciples. Some of us are called to do this as our full-time vocation, but most of us are called to do this with the people where we live and work in our everyday lives.

Are you a disciple? Who is helping you follow Jesus? Are you a disciple-maker? Who are you helping to follow Jesus?

Reflect and Respond
What is Jesus saying to me right now?

What step of faith is Jesus calling me to take today?

DAY 11

READ AND LISTEN: MARK 3:20-30
Take a minute to listen for what the Spirit is saying in these verses...

COMMENT AND CONSIDER
In many ways Jesus was a typical first-century Galilean Jew. He grew up in a small Jewish village. After attending elementary school (Hebrew: *Beth Sefer*) until the age of 12, Jesus worked in the family business as a builder for 18 years. He observed the Sabbath, worshiped in the synagogue, and made annual pilgrimages to Jerusalem for the Passover. We could compare him to countless other men of his age.

But in other ways Jesus was very unusual. His birth was attended by mysterious events. By the age of twelve, Jesus was smarter than the greatest teachers of his time. Although he was the eldest, Jesus did not marry but left his extended family home at the age of 30. Although he had not been formally trained in the rabbinical traditions, he was recognized as a rabbi and invited to teach in synagogues wherever he went. Jesus referred to God as his own Father and spoke directly as his representative. He had supernatural insights about people he could not have known, humanly speaking. He demonstrated the power of God to cure the sick, heal the broken, and cast out demons with a simple command.

It is not surprising that the religious scribes were deeply threatened by Jesus' wisdom, authority, and power. They claimed a superior knowledge of God's will and sought to impose a system of religious rules that Jesus openly rejected. Jesus demonstrated a wisdom and insight about God's will that profoundly transcended their banal legalism. Even more, Jesus' spiritual authority and power were on a completely different plane than anything these religious teachers had ever experienced.

We tend to fear things we don't understand, especially if they are powerful. That is why the religious leaders accused Jesus of being possessed by

"*Beelzebul*," the prince of demons. A later rabbinic tradition recorded in the Mishnah describes Jesus in similar terms, "On the eve of Passover they hanged Yeshu [Jesus]. And an announcer went out, in front of him, for fourteen days [saying]: 'He is going to be stoned because he practiced sorcery.'" There could be no greater misrepresentation of Jesus' identity and ministry than this.

Jesus responded by pointing out the inherent contradiction of attributing to demons the very power he used to cast out demons. That would be like a king waging war against himself! Jesus asked, *"How can Satan drive out Satan?"* and then told a parable about a thief seeking to plunder a strong man's house. The only way to steal from a strong man is to first subdue him so you can take his possessions. Obviously, the strong man represents the demons who have taken possession of God's children. Jesus was "stealing" them back by subduing the demons in the power of God and casting them out.

The scribes made the fatal error of failing to recognize the power and presence of God in Jesus. By identifying God's power with demons, they fundamentally positioned themselves in opposition to God. It is similar to the mistake of another Pharisee named Saul, who thought he was doing God's will by persecuting the followers of Jesus, but then discovered he was actually opposing the God he sought to serve. The key difference between Saul and these scribes is that Saul was willing to humble himself, let go of his privileged religious status, and embrace the truth when confronted by Jesus. These religious leaders simply hardened their resolve to destroy Jesus. This is the only sin God can't forgive: the refusal to recognize Jesus for who he is and submit to him.

Have you ever been confronted by the truth of Jesus? How did you respond? How are you responding right now?

Reflect and Respond

What is Jesus saying to me right now?

What step of faith is Jesus calling me to take today?

DAY 12

READ AND LISTEN: MARK 3:31-35
Take a minute to listen for what the Spirit is saying in these verses…

COMMENT AND CONSIDER
Although the religious teachers attributed Jesus' surprising words and powerful actions to demons, his family back in Nazareth had a different reaction. Bewildered by the sensational reports they heard about Jesus, they assumed *"He's out of his mind."* (Mark 3:20) Every time Jesus returned to Capernaum, the large courtyard of Simon and Andrew's house filled up with people from all kinds of different backgrounds. This was so far outside the norms of the conservative religious culture in which Jesus was raised that it seemed to them Jesus had gone off the deep end.

People in biblical times normally lived in extended family homes built around a central courtyard with a strong outer wall and door. Their families were typically made up of multiple generations of both blood and non-blood relationships: grandparents, parents, aunts and uncles, siblings and cousins, people who worked in the family business and slaves. The function of a large family and a strong home (Greek: *oikos*) was to protect the family and provide for the family, which is why people always lived in an *oikos* if they could. This has been the case throughout history in nearly every culture until modern times. The idea of living only as a nuclear family with just a mom, a dad, and some kids, is a modern, western aberration.

This means the *oikos* was focused on what was good for the members of the family. It was an inward-focused system. In an honor/shame culture, this meant you only invited people into your *oikos* who would bring honor to the family. You would not invite in people who could bring shame. The fact that Jesus, as the oldest son of a family whose father had most likely died, had left his own *oikos* in Nazareth was the first shock. But now they heard he was welcoming into his new *oikos* the sick and the lame, prostitutes and demon-possessed people. To top it off he claimed to speak for God and was purported to perform miracles!

The religious leaders condemned Jesus and plotted to kill him. But his mother Mary was so distraught for her son that she gathered Jesus' brothers and his sisters and set off for Capernaum to find Jesus and bring him home to Nazareth where they could nurse him back to health. When they arrived at Simon and Andrew's home, the courtyard was full of people, as usual. Standing at the outer door, they asked the crowd to convey the word to Jesus that his family had arrived and was asking for him. The message was passed from person to person until it reached Jesus inside the house.

When he heard it, Jesus looked at the men and women who were seated around him and said, *"Who are my mother and my brothers? … "Here are my mother and my brothers! Whoever does the will of God is my brother and sister and mother."* With this simple statement, Jesus redefined what family is meant to be. He was not rejecting his biological family, but he made it clear they would not define family for him. Jesus was building a new kind of family. Not just a biological family, but a spiritual family. Not just a nuclear family, but an extended family. Not a family that is focused on itself, but a family that is focused on doing the will of God on earth as it is done in heaven. This is a family defined by the Kingdom of God. This is a family on mission.

What defines your family? Are you willing to follow Jesus' example and welcome people of different backgrounds into your home? What would it mean to build a Jesus-shaped family on mission?

Reflect and Respond

What is Jesus saying to me right now?

What step of faith is Jesus calling me to take today?

Footsteps Every Week: Review

Write a brief summary of what Jesus said to you each day this past week and the step of faith he called you to take:

Monday

Tuesday

Wednesday

Thursday

Friday

Saturday

Footsteps Every Week: Reflect

Big Picture
As you look over what Jesus has said to you this past week, do you see any themes? What is the most important thing you need to remember and believe?

Predictable Pattern
As you look over what Jesus called you to do this past week, is there a new predictable pattern he is inviting you to establish in your life with God and others?

Plant the Word
As you look over the readings from this past week, write out the passage that feels most important for you and memorize it over the next week:

DAY 13

READ AND LISTEN: MARK 4:1-20
Take a minute to listen for what the Spirit is saying in these verses…

COMMENT AND CONSIDER

As usual, Jesus was attracting huge crowds, so to avoid the crush and reflect his voice to more people, he asked Simon to use his boat and to row out into "Sower's Cove," just west of Capernaum, so he could teach. Audiological tests in this cove have determined that a person speaking in a boat there could be heard by more than 5,000 people seated on the curved hillside. To commemorate this event, a recently built chapel facing the lake in nearby Magdala has a platform designed to blend into the waters of the lake behind it and a pulpit shaped like a boat from which the preaching is done!

Jesus often told parables, which are short stories drawn from everyday life with deeper meanings that can only be found by wrestling with the story. Jesus' parables were designed to draw people into the Good News of the Kingdom and often had paradoxical, humorous, or even shocking twists that made people think more deeply about their implications. They were also easily passed on to others by everyday people.

Farmers in first-century Palestine lived in villages and worked their fields in the countryside surrounding their village. This meant hardened paths typically ran alongside or even through farmers' fields. Most of the land of Israel is comprised of a relatively thin layer of fertile soil spread across a limestone bedrock. Normally a farmer plowed his field and then planted the seed. Some crops could be planted one seed at a time directly in the ploughed furrows, but a field of grain was typically planted by broadcast sowing, in which the farmer simply scattered seed evenly across the entire field.

Jesus' parable pictures a farmer casting seed across his field of varying terrain. The seed lands on four types of soil: hardened, shallow, weed-infested, and good. The seed has differing outcomes in each type of soil.

On the hardened path, it is stolen by birds before it can even sprout. On the shallow soil, it springs up quickly but can't put down roots because the bedrock is immediately beneath the surface. On the weedy soil, it sprouts and grows but can't get enough water and nutrients because it must compete with the opportunistic thorns. The result in all these cases is that the seed does not accomplish its purpose which is to multiply good fruit.

The good soil receives the seed and allows the roots to go deep, so the plants can grow and endure adverse conditions. This means each seed that takes root in the good soil fulfills its purpose of multiplication. Ancient writers indicate that seeds planted in fertile soil could produce stalks with 30-100 grains, which is the range of multiplication Jesus described. To some degree the farmer doesn't know which part of his field will bring such a good return. He has to sow the seed across the whole field and then see where it takes root and bears fruit.

When Jesus trained the disciples in his missional methodology, he told them to *"offer your peace"* in each town they visited. Then he instructed them to build relationships with those who were receptive and responsive by spending time with them and sharing meals together. These were the "people of peace" with whom they were to then demonstrate the Kingdom of God and explain the Good News. (See Matthew 10 and Luke 10.) Jesus' call to *"repent and believe"* is a call to be receptive and responsive. People of peace are good soil who will receive our offer of friendship and reciprocate. When we sow Good News into them, it takes root, multiplies, and bears good fruit. This is how the Kingdom of God comes.

What does it look like for you to be good soil? Who are the receptive and responsive people in whom you are sowing Kingdom seed?

Reflect and Respond

What is Jesus saying to me right now?

What step of faith is Jesus calling me to take today?

DAY 14

READ AND LISTEN: MARK 4:10-20
Take a minute to listen for what the Spirit is saying in these verses…

COMMENT AND CONSIDER

Parables are different than allegories. An allegory tends to make a direct symbolic association between the features of the story and situations in the real world. A parable tends to be a story with a main point that can then be applied to life in the real world. Some of Jesus' parables are simple, one-point stories, like the woman sweeping for a lost coin. The story shows us God cares about every person who is lost and is actively seeking for them to be found. To understand this parable's meaning, we don't need to allegorize the story by saying the woman represents God, the broom represents the church, the cracks in the floor represent temptations of this world, etc.

Even if they are not allegories, Jesus' parables do not always have as straightforward a meaning as we might assume. They are designed to make the hearers wrestle with the meaning and implications of the Good News of the Kingdom. Like Jacob at Peniel, those who must wrestle with God discover who they are and why they are here. This is how we see the face of God and live. (See Genesis 32:24-32.) Even Jesus' closest disciples had to wrestle with the parables he told and did not immediately understand them. On one occasion they waited until they were alone with Jesus, and then they asked him to explain the parable of the seed and the four different soils.

Jesus responded by making a distinction between those who follow him and the crowds. The crowds hear Jesus' parables, but those who are close to him gain deeper insights into *"the secret of the kingdom of God."* The word translated *"secret"* in this passage is the Greek word *musterion*, the word for "mystery," which is insight or knowledge that can only come through divine revelation. As Jesus explained this parable to the disciples, he revealed its meaning and made the mystery of the Kingdom intelligible to them.

Then Jesus quoted an enigmatic verse from Isaiah 6:9-10, which comes immediately after Isaiah accepts God's call to go and represent him to the people. At first reading it seems as though God is trying to prevent people from understanding and responding to his word. With deeper study, however, it becomes clear that God called Isaiah to proclaim his word to the people so it would reveal who was open and receptive and who was not.

It is disciples who gain the insights needed to follow Jesus. If we remain at a distance, his words will remain a mystery to us and we will fulfill Isaiah's prophecy that *"they may indeed look, and yet not perceive; they may indeed listen, and yet not understand."* Obviously, Jesus wants everyone to see and understand him, but parables become one of the ways the wheat is distinguished from the chaff. They reveal who is willing to wrestle with God and draw near to Jesus and who insists on keeping God at arm's distance and blending into the crowd. Those who draw near will see and understand.

On his last night with the disciples before his arrest, Jesus said, *"I still have many things to tell you, but you can't bear them now. When the Spirit of truth comes, he will guide you into all the truth."* (John 16:12-13) As we read the parables today, Jesus is still present to us in the power of his Spirit, and we can wrestle with him until we gain the insight we need into the mystery of the Kingdom of God. Are you willing to draw near to Jesus? Are you willing to wrestle with his words?

Reflect and Respond

What is Jesus saying to me right now?

What step of faith is Jesus calling me to take today?

DAY 15

READ AND LISTEN: MARK 4:21-34
Take a minute to listen for what the Spirit is saying in these verses…

COMMENT AND CONSIDER
Before the invention of electric lights, human life was governed by the rising and setting of the sun. People generally rose with the sun and went to sleep after sunset, because darkness prevented most activity. The only way to constructively use those hours after sunset and before sleep was with firelight. Candles were expensive and rare, so most people used clay lamps which contained a reservoir for olive oil and held a wick which was lit. These small lamps were normally set in recessed niches in the stone walls of a room or set up on a free-standing lampstand so the light could illuminate a larger area.

Jesus continued his theme of revelation by comparing his parables to oil lamps that reveal what is otherwise hidden. Eventually the truth of his words will become evident to everyone, but for now his teaching will only bring light to those who will receive it. Everyone has ears, but those who are willing to use their ears to hear what he is saying will be like someone in a dark room who lights a lamp and suddenly sees what is in the room.

Jesus went on to tell simple parables of the Kingdom. *"By the measure you use, it will be measured to you—and more will be added to you."* If you use a big scoop, a big scoop will be used for you. The degree to which you put into practice the truths Jesus offers is the degree to which you will receive more insight. This is why those who receive what is given will receive even more abundant life, whereas those who persist in closing their ears and hardening their hearts will actually become even more lost and confused.

Then Jesus gave another picture of how the Kingdom of God works. When seeds are scattered on fertile soil they take root, sprout, grow, and produce fruit, but the farmer doesn't know how it actually works. It's a mystery! That is the case with the Kingdom. We can scatter the seed. We can receive the seed. But it is a mystery how the word of the Kingdom takes root in our hearts, transforms our lives, and multiplies goodness in the lives of others. This is the hidden work of God's Spirit.

In a third parable Jesus compares the Kingdom of God to the proverbially tiny mustard seed. Just as there is a disproportionate relationship between the size of the seed and the large plant that grows from it, the same is true in God's Kingdom where little things can produce huge results. In the kingdoms of this world, the big, splashy things get attention and priority. In the Kingdom of God, the little things no one knows about often have a surprisingly big impact. Like a widow dropping her two pennies into the Temple treasury. Or someone offering a cup of cold water to *"one of these little ones."* Or a woman touching the hem of Jesus' robe. (See Mark 5:27-29; 12:41-43; Matthew 10:42.)

When you faithfully put into practice the truth Jesus offers, he gives you more and a lamp is lit in a dark room. When you do something small out of great love, amazing things happen, and another lamp is lit in that dark room. There is no human explanation for how the Kingdom grows and bears fruit in your life. It is the mysterious work of God that you can't explain but can only participate in. When you do, another lamp is lit in your dark room. What lamps need to be lit in your dark room?

REFLECT AND RESPOND

What is Jesus saying to me right now?

What step of faith is Jesus calling me to take today?

DAY 16

READ AND LISTEN: MARK 4:35-41

Take a minute to listen for what the Spirit is saying in these verses…

COMMENT AND CONSIDER

In January 1986, a drought on the Sea of Galilee revealed the remains of an ancient fishing boat buried in the lakebed. After years of painstaking restoration, the boat can now be viewed and studied. It is 27 feet long, 8 feet wide, 4.6 feet deep, had fore and aft decks, could be rowed or sailed with a stepped mast. It held a crew of five plus ten passengers and dates from the first century. It is exactly the kind of boat Jesus' fishing disciples used in support of his mission. After a time of teaching beside the lake, Jesus and his disciples sailed to the other side, and a major storm hit them.

The Sea of Galilee is a beautiful freshwater lake that sits in a deep depression of the Jordan Rift Valley, some 700 feet below sea level. The Jordanian highlands rise along the eastern shore of the lake and form the edge of a desert plateau stretching hundreds of miles further to the east. When the desert winds blow westward over this barren plateau, the hot air drops suddenly down onto the cool air rising off the lake creating violent and unpredictable storms.

On my very first visit to the Sea of Galilee, also in January 1986, a friend and I saw such a storm suddenly form on the eastern side of the lake. The storm came racing across the water toward us, and we had to scramble off the rocks where we were sitting to escape the six-foot high waves that began battering the shore! This is the kind of storm that sent waves breaking over the boat and began to sink it. Meanwhile, Jesus was asleep underneath the rear deck on a *"pillow."* It was common to place sandbags in the bottom of a boat for ballast, and they were sometimes referred to as "pillows."

At least four of Jesus' twelve closest disciples were seasoned fishermen who had earned their living sailing these waters nearly every day. Their accusatory question reveals the depth of their fear and the severity of the storm, *"Teacher! Don't you care that we're going to die?"* The contrast between their fear and Jesus' peaceful slumber is almost laughable. Here we see both Jesus' full humanity in his physical exhaustion, and his profound faith in the Father to whom he has completely entrusted his life. Jesus didn't carry out his mission with some kind of divine power to which we do not have access. On the contrary, Jesus set an example for us by walking just as we do and accomplishing everything he did by faith in his heavenly Father and the power of the Spirit within him.

Roused from slumber by the cries of his disciples, Jesus finally got up and rebuked the wind and waves, *"Silence! Be still!"* Notice how Jesus exercised the authority given to him. He did not ask his heavenly Father to still the storm, but rather directly commanded the storm to cease. This is the authority of someone who knows his Father is the King of the universe. This is someone through whom the power of that King flowed to carry out the will of God. At this word the storm suddenly ceased, and the lake became perfectly still. The disciples recognized the connection between Jesus' identity and power when they expressed their amazement by asking, *"Who then is this? Even the wind and the sea obey him!"*

Jesus told them the key to exercising this kind of power is the intentional exercise of faith. When we know our Father is the King of kings, and we begin to believe that being a son or daughter of the King means we have been given divine authority to carry out his will, our perspective changes. We can learn how to operate as conduits of God's power when we submit to his will, exercise his authority, and let the Holy Spirit guide our words and actions. This is how Jesus rebuked the wind and waves and ended the deadly storm.

What storms threaten you and those you love? What authority do you carry by virtue of your identity? How can you learn to exercise that authority by faith to do God's will?

Reflect and Respond

What is Jesus saying to me right now?

What step of faith is Jesus calling me to take today?

DAY 17

READ AND LISTEN: MARK 5:1-20
Take a minute to listen for what the Spirit is saying in these verses...

COMMENT AND CONSIDER

The west side of the Sea of Galilee was primarily inhabited by Jews, while the eastern side of the lake was dominated by the large Gentile cities of the Decapolis. The Decapolis was a league of ten powerful Greek cities that controlled the territory around their walls and had made a treaty with one another and with Rome. This allowed them to operate somewhat independently but with the assurance of security. There were several of these Greek cities on the eastern side of the lake including Hippos, Gadara, Gergesa, and Gerasa.

There is some confusion about which region of these latter three cities Jesus and the disciples traveled into, but in any case, it is clear they were entering Gentile territory. Jesus cast a universal vision in which people of every nation are welcomed into the Kingdom of God, but he strategically focused his mission on the Jewish peasants of Galilee whom he called *"the lost sheep of the house of Israel."* (Matthew 10:5-6) By sailing to the area of the Decapolis, he intentionally went outside his primary mission field.

When Jesus and the disciples arrived on the eastern shore, they immediately encountered a man who was so deeply demonized that he was robbed of nearly all his humanity, living and acting like a wild animal. He had been exiled to the tombs and chained to the rocks to no avail, and with demonic strength he subjected himself to the violence his isolation prevented him from inflicting on others. But at the sight of Jesus, this terrorized and terrifying man ran and knelt at his feet, crying out, *"What do you have to do with me, Jesus, Son of the Most High God."*

As Jesus began to confront the powers of darkness that held this man hostage, he demanded to know the demon's name. In the ancient world it was understood that using a person's name gave you power over them.

This may be why demons so often cried out identifying titles when they met Jesus, because they were trying in vain to counter his authority and power. In this case, the demonizing presence identified itself by saying, *"My name is Legion, because we are many."* Although Jesus was confronting an army of demons, the authority he wielded as Son of the King was so great that they were already begging Jesus for mercy. This is the same authority we have been given as sons and daughters of our heavenly Father, the King of kings.

The large herd of pigs grazing on the hillside nearby was a vivid reminder they were no longer in Jewish territory but deep in the Gentile Decapolis. From a Jewish perspective, it is ironically apropos for these unclean spirits to ask Jesus to cast them into this herd, since pigs are considered ritually unclean. Jesus cast the legion of demons out of this man and into the pigs, and it was poetic justice when they suddenly committed mass suicide! From a Middle Eastern perspective, this is a classic story of a wise man cleverly tricking his nemesis into suffering at the hands of his own evil plot.

The transformation of this liberated man was profound. The same calm Jesus brought to the stormy lake had now fallen over this tormented soul. Now he was completely sane and articulate, and his only desire was to follow and serve Jesus. Knowing this Gentile would have a very hard time connecting with the Jews in their primary mission field, Jesus instead commissioned him as a missionary to his own Greek culture and sent him to share the Good News of the Kingdom in the Decapolis!

Have you identified your missional target as Jesus did? How has Jesus commissioned and sent you as a missionary to the people in your context? How are you learning to share the Good News with people in that cultural mission field?

Reflect and Respond

What is Jesus saying to me right now?

What step of faith is Jesus calling me to take today?

DAY 18

READ AND LISTEN: MARK 5:21-34
Take a minute to listen for what the Spirit is saying in these verses…

COMMENT AND CONSIDER

The Old Testament Law identified certain things that rendered a person ritually unclean if they touched them. These included touching a corpse, a person with a skin rash, a house with mold, or eating pork. This was not a moral judgment; it was reminder for God's people that they were to live in a way that was distinct from the pagan cultures that surrounded them. But a person who contracted ritual impurity was considered separated from God and was isolated from their community until they could restore their purity status. For this reason, religious Jews took ritual purity very seriously.

Leviticus identifies a woman's uterine bleeding as a source of uncleanness. Not only was a bleeding woman considered unclean, but anyone who touched her was unclean, anything she touched was unclean, and anyone who touched something she sat on was unclean. This meant that a woman's monthly menstrual cycle required her to separate herself from everyone for seven days. (See Leviticus 15:19-33.)

Mark tells us about a woman who had experienced uterine bleeding for twelve years, which meant she was considered continually ritually impure. This required her not only to distance herself from her community, but to separate herself from her own family and stay confined to her own quarters. She was not allowed to participate in any religious festivals or enter the Temple to worship God. Although these were not moral issues, a sense of shame was heaped on the one who was considered impure, and especially on a woman. On top of this, she had spent her entire life savings hiring physicians to treat her condition. Now she was not only alone in her shame but also in poverty.

This desperate woman had heard of Jesus' power to heal, and she knew he was her last and best hope for restoration to health, family, and community. However, she also knew she was forbidden to mix with other people in public places, much less approach a rabbi who was considered a holy man. And so, this unnamed woman of incredible courage and strength decided she would try to approach Jesus secretly while he made his way through the crowd, hoping to maintain her anonymity. She pressed through the throngs of people trying to get close to Jesus, reached out from behind him, and touched the fringe of his robe.

When she touched his robe, Jesus was immediately aware that the power of God had flowed through him into another person, and he asked who had touched him. Here we see Jesus was not operating in his own divine omniscience, but rather in his full humanity as a conduit of the Holy Spirit who was guiding him by faith. The woman knew she could no longer hide in the crowd, so she came forward knowing full well that Jesus had every right to publicly denounce her for passing impurity on to him. To her shock Jesus did exactly the opposite. He publicly affirmed her as a member of God's family and praised her for an act of courageous faith. *"Daughter," he said to her, "your faith has saved you. Go in peace and be healed from your affliction."* In that moment her whole life was changed, and she was restored to her family and the family of God!

Do you feel unworthy to ask Jesus for what you need from him? What would it take for you to press through the obstacles that keep you from drawing closer to Jesus? How can you remove those kinds of obstacles for others?

Reflect and Respond
What is Jesus saying to me right now?

What step of faith is Jesus calling me to take today?

Footsteps Every Week: Review

Write a brief summary of what Jesus said to you each day this past week and the step of faith he called you to take:

Monday

Tuesday

Wednesday

Thursday

Friday

Saturday

Footsteps Every Week: Reflect

Big Picture
As you look over what Jesus has said to you this past week, do you see any themes? What is the most important thing you need to remember and believe?

Predictable Pattern
As you look over what Jesus called you to do this past week, is there a new predictable pattern he is inviting you to establish in your life with God and others?

Plant the Word
As you look over the readings from this past week, write out the passage that feels most important for you and memorize it over the next week:

DAY 19

READ AND LISTEN: MARK 5:35-43

Take a minute to listen for what the Spirit is saying in these verses...

COMMENT AND CONSIDER

Each local synagogue was run by a group of elders known as "synagogue rulers." These men of considerable social status and power organized the Sabbath prayer services, scheduled rabbis to teach, and managed the synagogue finances. In the previous passage, we met a man named Jairus, who held this position in his synagogue. Despite the growing tension between Jesus and the religious leaders, Jairus came to him in public, fell down before him, and begged for help. *"My little daughter is dying. Come and lay your hands on her so that she can get well and live."* (Mark 5:23)

On the way to help this girl, Jesus encountered the brave hemorrhaging woman. Just after Jesus healed her, Jairus received the news every parent dreads most, *"Your daughter is dead."* Although his servants and the crowd assumed there was no point in bothering Jesus anymore, Jesus simply told Jairus, *"Don't be afraid. Only believe."* The word *"believe"* here is the verbal form of the noun translated *"faith."* Paul tells us *"faith comes from hearing, and hearing through the word of Christ."* (Romans 10:17) Jesus spoke faith into this man's heart and now, in the face of his greatest fear, Jesus called him to exercise that faith against all odds.

In the first century, Jews normally buried the deceased before sunset on the day of their death. In Middle Eastern culture, grief is not a private affair, but something loudly and publicly expressed. For this reason, it was common to hire people who specialized in demonstrative expressions of mourning to help you honor the dead. When Jesus and Jairus arrived at Jairus' house, the professional mourners had already gathered to wail and weep. Jesus told them their theatrics were unnecessary because the child was only asleep, but they just laughed at him.

Mark tells us Jesus kicked the professional mourners out and specifically invited the child's parents and his four closest disciples to join him in the room where the girl's body lay. Jesus was removing the skeptics and building an atmosphere of faith in order to carry out the most difficult of all healings, bringing someone who has died back to life. It is good to remember this is different than Jesus' own resurrection. He was transformed into his new body as the first fruit of the new creation, gloriously transformed, fully alive, never to die again, and soon to ascend into heaven. When Jesus raised this little girl and Lazarus, they returned to their former state of life with imperfect bodies that would eventually die again.

Even so, this greatest of earthly miracles was carried out by faith. Jesus invited those closest to him and to the girl to join him in exercising the faith it takes to resuscitate the dead. Most first-century exorcists and healers used complex spells and esoteric rituals in their attempts to exercise power. By contrast, Jesus' deliverance and healing ministry was a simple exercise of faith and authority. He simply said, *"Talitha koum" (which is translated, "Little girl, I say to you, get up")* The parents and disciples could hardly believe what they witnessed. Jesus asked them to keep it quiet in an effort to avoid provoking the religious authorities to shut him down before he could accomplish all the Father was calling him to do.

If Jesus asked other people to join him in exercising faith for healing, how much more do we need each other when it comes to exercising faith? When we share testimony of God's power, our collective faith grows stronger. When we exercise faith together, it reinforces our faith and multiplies the fruit. With whom can you share a testimony of what God has done lately? Who are you going to invite to join you in exercising faith?

REFLECT AND RESPOND

What is Jesus saying to me right now?

What step of faith is Jesus calling me to take today?

DAY 20

READ AND LISTEN: MARK 6:1-6
Take a minute to listen for what the Spirit is saying in these verses…

COMMENT AND CONSIDER
In first-century culture, your extended family of origin was the foundation of your life. It protected you from danger and exploitation. It was your source of the food, water, education, and community you needed. It was where the men apprenticed into the family trade and the women learned to run the family business. Your extended family was your identity and the basis of your honor in your society.

When Jesus returned to his hometown of Nazareth, he brought honor to his extended family. Their family business was construction—the word typically translated *"carpenter"* actually means "builder." Although Jesus was a builder and was not formally trained as a teacher, he was recognized as a rabbi because of the authority of his teaching and ministry. In fact, the synagogue rulers asked Jesus to teach in the synagogue service that Sabbath. When Jesus began to teach about the coming messianic age, people were amazed that this boy they had watched grow up was now a powerful teacher. But as Jesus cast the vision of an inclusive Kingdom where even Gentiles were welcomed into the family of God, the mood of the crowd grew sour. They reminded each other he was only one of six or more children of Mary. They pointed out his lack of official training. They highlighted the fact that he made his living with his hands, not his mind or his mouth. How dare Jesus include the Gentiles! Who does he think he is? As Mark says, *they were offended by him.*

Usually, people were amazed at Jesus' authority and power, but this time it was his turn to be amazed at their lack of faith in him. It had had a direct impact on his ability to heal. This is another reminder that Jesus didn't heal people out of his own divinity, but in his full humanity. He exercised faith in the authority given to him by his Father the King, and that is how the supernatural power of God flowed through him to do God's will. But due to the lack of receptive, trusting hearts in Nazareth, Jesus was not able to see the same breakthrough in healing there that he did elsewhere.

It wasn't just the people of Nazareth who didn't believe in Jesus and rejected his vision of the Kingdom of God. Jesus' extended family didn't stand with him when the crowd turned ugly. They didn't embrace his vision either. As Jesus said, *"A prophet is not without honor except in his hometown, among his relatives, and in his household."* The Greek word translated *"household"* here is *oikos,* that word for extended family. It is no accident that Jesus left Nazareth and joined the *oikos* of Simon and Andrew in Capernaum. He knew he needed an extended family who believed in him, embraced his vision of the Kingdom, and would stand with him in the face of opposition.

We all need a solid base from which to operate. We need a safe place where we know we are loved as we are, where people believe in our potential. We need a place where we can be nurtured, trained, and equipped for the calling God has put on our life. We need a place where we can invest in others and invite them to follow our example. We need an extended spiritual family that is following Jesus on mission together.

Who is your spiritual family? How does your natural family overlap with that family? What can you do to strengthen your base of operations?

Reflect and Respond
What is Jesus saying to me right now?

What step of faith is Jesus calling me to take today?

DAY 21

READ AND LISTEN: MARK 6:7-13
Take a minute to listen for what the Spirit is saying in these verses…

COMMENT AND CONSIDER
When Jesus called people saying, *"Follow me,"* they understood he was calling them into a discipling relationship. It was not just an invitation to listen to his teaching and witness his miracles. It was an invitation to stay close enough so they not only heard his words and learned to know what he knew, but could also watch his ways and learn to do what he did. Ultimately, their goal was to live a Jesus-shaped life and make disciples as he did.

So it was no surprise that Jesus began to prepare the disciples to go out and do all the things they had been watching him do. This was the natural next step in their journey of discipleship. Jesus explicitly authorized them to do what they had seen him doing. Then he told them to travel extremely light. It is counterintuitive to set out on a missional journey with no food or money or extra supplies, but Jesus intentionally put them in a place where they had to trust God and rely on others to help them.

Jesus told them to take a highly relational approach to their mission. They were not to go alone, but to go with a partner. They were not to gather large crowds but look for friends who would invite them into their extended family homes. Then they were to stay with them, investing in those relationships. There is something about eating meals and sharing life together that opens people to seeing and hearing the Good News.

Their message was that *"people should repent."* The Greek word for *"repent"* is *metanoia*, which literally means "a change of mind." In this context it means to let God give you a new Kingdom perspective by listening to his Word and responding to his Spirit. But he also called them to demonstrate the Kingdom by to casting out demons and healing the sick. When people get to know us and believe that we care about them, when they see us use the power of God to bless and heal people, and when they hear the Good News of the Kingdom from us, they are often moved to repent, to trust Jesus, and start living as a part of his Kingdom. This is the missional strategy of Jesus.

Jesus also taught his disciples not to invest time and energy into people who were not open to them or receptive to their message. He used the image of shaking the dust off our feet, a picture of letting go and moving on. When we offer our friendship and that friendship is not reciprocated, we can simply move on to the next person or family or community and offer our friendship there instead. If we keep doing that, eventually we will find those who are receptive, and we can invest in those friendships until we see people come to faith and begin to follow Jesus.

It is such a relief to know we don't need to stand on a street corner trying to pressure strangers to believe in Jesus. All we need to do is look for friends, be vulnerable enough to let them help us, show them what the Kingdom of God looks like, and then tell them the Good News. It doesn't take a seminary degree or a special commission to be a missionary; it just takes following the example and teaching of Jesus!

Are you living your life on mission as Jesus and his first followers did? Are you offering your friendship to those who don't yet know Jesus? If so, what is your next step in showing and sharing Good News with them?

Reflect and Respond

What is Jesus saying to me right now?

What step of faith is Jesus calling me to take today?

DAY 22

READ AND LISTEN: MARK 6:14-29

Take a minute to listen for what the Spirit is saying in these verses…

COMMENT AND CONSIDER

Herod the Great ruled Israel on behalf of the Romans when Jesus was born. Herod had ten wives and numerous sons, so the family tree can get a little confusing. The *"King Herod"* referred to in this passage is one of his sons, Herod Antipas, who ruled Galilee during the ministry of Jesus. As Jesus' popularity grew, so did the rumors about him. Some said he was the great prophet like Moses foretold in Deuteronomy 18:15-19. Others thought he was Elijah returned from heaven as prophesied in Malachi 4:5-6. Still others wondered if John the Baptist had come back from the dead. It was this last suggestion that haunted Herod Antipas.

When Jesus' followers started doing the same things Jesus did, it became apparent to Antipas this was becoming a movement that threatened his power. His guilt over the death of John the Baptist filled him with fear that Jesus was "John 2.0"! This prompted Mark to give us a flashback to explain what led Antipas to execute John.

Antipas had two brothers named Philip. Philip the Tetrarch ruled the area to the northeast of Galilee, called the Golan Heights today. Another brother named Herod Philip lived as a private citizen back in Rome where most of Herod's sons were educated. This Philip was married to Herodias, a granddaughter of Herod the Great, Philip's half-niece. When Antipas visited Rome and stayed with Philip, he fell in love with his sister-in-law Herodias, also his half-niece, and promptly asked her to marry him. She agreed on the condition that Antipas divorce his current wife, who was the daughter of Aretas IV, king of the Nabateans. Antipas agreed and divorced his wife, which led to a devastating war in which King Aretas dealt Antipas a humiliating military loss.

Meanwhile, back home John the Baptist began to speak out against this divorce and remarriage because marrying your brother's wife is forbidden in Leviticus 18:16. John's public rebuke of Antipas and Herodias led to his arrest and confinement in the massive desert fortress called Machaerus on the east side of the Dead Sea. Although Herodias wanted to execute John, Mark tells us Antipas protected John because he recognized him as a holy and righteous man. Antipas even liked to call him out of prison for private conversations.

Later, Antipas threw a lavish birthday party for himself, demonstrating his pagan lifestyle because religious Jews did not celebrate birthdays. Furthermore, the men were in a separate dining hall from the women while the young daughter of Herodias was dancing seductively for the men. (See verse 24 in which Salome had to leave the dining hall to confer with her mother.) The exaggerated promise of *"anything up to half my kingdom"* implies Antipas was thoroughly inebriated. Recent excavations of the Machaerus fortress have revealed it contained two banquet halls, one larger and one smaller, which perfectly fits Mark's account.

Herodias saw her opportunity to eliminate a political rival and instructed her daughter to ask for John's head on a platter. Antipas grudgingly agreed because he had sworn a binding oath to the girl. The whole grisly account is a vivid reminder of the violence and injustice unleashed when corrupt people are given nearly unchecked power.

Antipas' paranoid fears that John had come back to haunt him arose after Jesus' disciples returned from their successful mission trip. It is one thing to have a charismatic leader threaten the status quo. There is a simple solution to this problem: eliminate the charismatic leader. However, if that leader is able to multiply him or herself in the lives of others who can do the same, it becomes an unstoppable force that even the most corrupted power cannot stop.

This is why the Romans, the Herodians, the Sadducees, and the Pharisees together could not stop the movement Jesus started—because his followers were empowered to do the same things he did. What about you? Are you learning to do what Jesus did? Are you passing that on to others who can do the same?

Reflect and Respond
What is Jesus saying to me right now?

What step of faith is Jesus calling me to take today?

DAY 23

READ AND LISTEN: MARK 6:30-44

Take a minute to listen for what the Spirit is saying in these verses…

COMMENT AND CONSIDER

Jesus modeled a healthy and fruitful rhythm and trained his disciples to imitate that way of life. He spent time alone with the Father in prayer each morning. He took 24 hours of rest for restoration and renewal each Sabbath day. After particularly busy seasons of ministry, he took the disciples away to a quiet spot on the lake for extra times of rest and refreshment. Between Capernaum and Magdala is a place beside the lake called Tabgha, which comes from the Greek word *heptapegon*, meaning "seven springs." It is a lush and beautiful spot because it is watered by seven strong springs which irrigate and cool the entire area. This seems to be one of the places where Jesus took his disciples for these seasonal local retreat days.

After the twelve disciples returned from their first mission trip without Jesus, he took them away by boat on one of these local retreats to rest and reflect on their experience. However, when they arrived, probably at Tabgha, the crowds had anticipated their plan and arrived ahead of them by land. Rather than drive all the people away, Jesus responded with compassion and decided to minister to them because he saw they were *"like sheep without a shepherd."*

Although Jesus already had a plan for this retreat, he was always open to what the Father was doing in the moment. He explained this posture when he said, *"Truly I tell you, the Son is not able to do anything on his own, but only what he sees the Father doing. For whatever the Father does, the Son likewise does these things."* (John 5:19) Jesus saw the Father was doing something with the crowd in that moment, so he set aside his plans and stepped into what he saw the Father doing. When you have regular predictable patterns of rest, it is easy to shift gears and follow the Spirit's guidance because you are not operating on the edge of burnout. Because Jesus had consistent rhythms of rest, he didn't have to be legalistic about his Sabbath day or other healthy rhythms in his life.

After spending the day teaching and ministering to the crowds, the disciples saw a crisis brewing. It was getting late, and the crowd was getting hungry, but they were not near any towns where people could buy food. The disciples approached Jesus and suggested he break up the gathering and send people to Capernaum or Magdala to buy food. Instead, Jesus challenged their faith when he responded, *"You give them something to eat."* Understandably, the disciples responded by pointing out the practical impossibility of such a plan. It would take eight month's wages to buy just a half a small loaf of bread for each of the men, not to mention their families! But Jesus was teaching them an important lesson.

He asked them, *"How many loaves do you have? Go and see."* They rummaged around and came back with the lunch of a small boy they found, five loaves and two fish. They were just 2,495 loaves short! It was obvious to the disciples that they were ridiculously under-resourced, but Jesus was about to show them how provision works in the Kingdom of God. He looked up to his Father, prayed over the tiny lunch, and gave a meager portion to each of the twelve disciples, sending them into the hungry crowd. And miraculously it was enough! More than enough. When they were finished everyone was full, and every disciple had more than they started with.

When you have a good Father who is the King of the Universe, he will always provide more than you need if you will step out in faith and follow Jesus' lead. In what way is God calling you to trust his provision today?

Reflect and Respond

What is Jesus saying to me right now?

What step of faith is Jesus calling me to take today?

DAY 24

READ AND LISTEN: MARK 6:45-56
Take a minute to listen for what God is saying in these verses…

COMMENT AND CONSIDER
After the hard work of ministering to the people all day and the excitement of the miraculous meal, Jesus dismissed the crowd and sent his disciples in a boat to Bethsaida on the *"other side"* of the lake while he took some time alone with the Father. Bethsaida (Hebrew: "house of the fisherman") was a Jewish fishing village on the north shore of the Sea of Galilee, just to the east of the place where the Jordan River entered the lake. It was the hometown of Jesus' disciple Philip and the birthplace of Simon and Andrew. During Jesus' ministry Herod Philip was in the process of raising the status of Bethsaida to a city and he gave it a Romanized name, Bethsaida-Julias. Recent excavations have confirmed the location of the city and uncovered a Roman bath there, evidence of Herod Philip's love for pagan culture.

Jesus went up on the hillside overlooking the lake, an area where he typically withdrew to be alone with the Father. After praying most of the night, from his vantage point Jesus could see the disciples out on the lake, but they were not making progress against the strong wind. There were four 3-hour-long night watches from 6 PM to 6 AM. The fourth watch was from 3 AM to 6 AM. And so, as dawn broke at the end of the fourth watch, Jesus came to the disciples walking on the water! After calming their fears, he joined them in the boat, the wind ceased, and they were astounded.

Mark's description of this miracle has two strange features. First, he writes that Jesus *"wanted to pass by them."* This seems odd if Jesus was going out to meet them on the water. Secondly, when Jesus tried to assuage their fears that he is not a ghost, he said, *"Have courage! It is I."* This final statement literally reads, *"I am."* In the Old Testament, when God appears to people, he is often said to *"pass by."* (See Exodus 34:61, Kings 19:11; Ezekiel 16:6-8, etc.) When God appeared to Moses in the burning bush, he told him his personal name, *"I AM WHO I AM."* (Exodus 3:14) It seems as if Jesus' appearance to the disciples as he walked on the water was meant to be a "theophany," an appearance of God, not unlike the glorious revelation on the Mount of Transfiguration. In Matthew's account of this incredible event, he concludes by telling us the disciples *"worshiped him and said, "Truly you are the Son of God."* (Matthew 14:33)

Surprisingly, Mark concludes his account of this event by telling us Jesus and the disciples landed their boat in Gennesaret, which is to the *west* of Tabgha and Capernaum, not *east* toward Bethsaida as they had originally planned. This means that after rowing hard all night, they ended up on the opposite shore from what they intended! And yet everywhere they went with Jesus, people's broken lives were made whole.

Do you ever feel like the wind is against you? Are you straining against the oars? Have you ended up in the opposite direction of where you were planning to go? If so, you are just like the disciples. And if you trust Jesus to meet you when the wind is against you and recognize that he is the Lord of the wind and the sea, he will show you the way no matter where you land. Is it time to stop trying so hard to row against the wind? Is it time to let Jesus get into the boat with you? How can you recognize Jesus' presence and invite him into your boat today?

Reflect and Respond

What is Jesus saying to me right now?

What step of faith is Jesus calling me to take today?

Footsteps Every Week: Review

Write a brief summary of what Jesus said to you each day this past week and the step of faith he called you to take:

Monday

Tuesday

Wednesday

Thursday

Friday

Saturday

Footsteps Every Week: Reflect

Big Picture

As you look over what Jesus has said to you this past week, do you see any themes? What is the most important thing you need to remember and believe?

Predictable Pattern

As you look over what Jesus called you to do this past week, is there a new predictable pattern he is inviting you to establish in your life with God and others?

Plant the Word

As you look over the readings from this past week, write out the passage that feels most important for you and memorize it over the next week:

Day 25

Read and Listen: Mark 7:1-8

Take a minute to listen for what the Spirit is saying in these verses…

Comment and Consider

When the people of Israel settled in the land of Canaan, they were surrounded by pagan nations whose practices were contrary to God's revealed will. To set his people apart from those unclean practices, God gave them a series of purity laws that symbolized their separation from pagan cultures. These involved ritual bathing, avoiding certain kinds of food and clothing, how they cut their hair and their beards, and what they could touch and not touch. These were not universally applicable moral principles, like murder or adultery; they were symbolic boundaries meant to help God's people avoid slipping into an immoral pagan lifestyle.

The Pharisees believed scrupulous observance of these symbolic boundaries was critical for living in a right relationship with God. They expanded on these rituals and added countless religious rules and practices to what was prescribed in the Law. These extra-biblical practices were sometimes called *"the traditions of the elders.* They also applied to everyday people the complex rituals which were prescribed for the priests when they were offering sacrifices in the Temple. They pictured every man as the priest of his family and every home as their own personal temple, therefore considered it mandatory to observe the extensive symbolic boundaries meant only for priests serving in the Temple.

The concept of ritual impurity was that you could contract this unseen condition by failing to observe these symbolic boundaries and rituals. This impurity could be contracted by touching an unclean person or by touching something an unclean person had touched. Some rabbis even taught that certain types of impurity could be transferred through the air by wind. It is similar to the way modern people think of germs, which can be passed without realizing it and have detrimental effects on unknowing victims.

For this reason, the Pharisees were quite aggressive in enforcing purity rules and separating themselves from anyone who might knowingly or unknowingly be ritually impure. They applied the "unclean" label to whole groups of people who they assumed would not be able to follow all these complex rules, such as shepherds who had to spend so much time out in the fields with their flocks. The result was a highly judgmental and exclusionary religious culture in which people were labeled and ranked based on their level of perceived "purity."

Jesus did not follow the Pharisaical rules and rituals. He followed the teaching of the Torah but clearly did not consider the extra-biblical traditions to be binding on him or his disciples. Where the Torah prescribed immersion in a ritual bath (Hebrew: *mikveh*) to be rid of ceremonial impurity, the Pharisees had created a whole series of handwashing rituals, particularly associated with meals. This was not to clean dirt off their hands but was purely for symbolic purposes. When the scribes and Pharisees came from Jerusalem to check out Jesus and his followers, they were shocked to see that they did not follow the proscribed handwashing ceremonies. When they confronted Jesus about this, he ignored the question and countered by confronting them with their religious hypocrisy, quoting Isaiah 29:13.

The word here translated *"hypocrites"* is the same word used to describe actors in the Greek theater. The Pharisees wore an external mask of religious piety, but their hearts were far from God. They were motivated more by the position and power they could gain through their system of religious rules than by actually loving God and serving his purpose.

Have any of your religious traditions become a reason to label or judge others? In what ways could you be hiding behind a veneer of religious piety to avoid addressing the more important matters of love, justice, and holiness? What is the hypocrisy the Spirit wants to root out of your heart so you can live a life of greater integrity?

Reflect and Respond

What is Jesus saying to me right now?

What step of faith is Jesus calling me to take today?

DAY 26

READ AND LISTEN: MARK 7:9-23
Take a minute to listen for what the Spirit is saying in these verses…

COMMENT AND CONSIDER

Jesus continued his criticism of the religious elite in Jerusalem by addressing the hypocrisy of imposing religious rules that hinder people from following the revealed will of God. God's command to *"honor your father and mother"* (Exodus 20:12) is important for children to learn when they are young, but it applies most of all to adult children as their parents age. First-century Jews considered it a sacred obligation to care for parents in their old age. However, Jesus pointed out that their rule about dedicated offerings to the Temple contradicted one of the Ten Commandments!

The rabbis taught you could dedicate certain portions of your property as a future gift to the Temple by declaring them *"corban."* This meant you could continue to use and benefit from that property until your death, at which time its ownership was transferred to the Temple hierarchy as a charitable donation. Jesus pointed out how this could be used as religious justification by adult children who failed to care for their elderly parents and support them financially, because they claimed all their assets were already "corban," dedicated to the Temple. It was completely backward to make these human religious rules more important than the revealed will of God in Scripture. As Jesus said, *"You nullify the word of God by your tradition that you have handed down."*

Then Jesus took his criticism of the ceremonial religious system one step further. Calling together a crowd of people, he told them, *"Nothing that goes into a person from outside can defile him, but the things that come out of a person are what defile him."* In one simple sentence, Jesus swept away the entire system of ritual purity! To make sure we understand what Jesus was saying, Mark adds the parenthetical statement, *"(Thus he declared all foods clean.)"* This may have been one of the most radical things Jesus ever said. Jesus made a critical distinction between the ceremonial rules of the Old Testament and the universally binding moral teachings of Scripture. He tells us the symbolic rules no longer apply in the Kingdom of God. Real impurity is a matter of the heart, not handwashing rituals!

By contrast Jesus pointed to the inward reality of human beings and what really matters. *"For from within, out of people's hearts, come evil thoughts, sexual immoralities, thefts, murders, adulteries, greed, evil actions, deceit, self-indulgence, envy, slander, pride, and foolishness."* What God cares about are the thoughts and attitudes deep inside a person which end up shaping their outward expressions and actions toward others. These things, said Jesus, defile a person or demonstrate their right relation to God. What matters is not outward observance of ritual purity, but inward development of moral purity that subsequently shapes and defines our outward lives.

This was such a radical shift that years later it precipitated a conflict among the apostles over whether Gentile believers in Jesus were required to follow all the ceremonial laws of the Old Testament, including circumcision. In the end, the Council of Jerusalem affirmed Jesus' statement that these symbolic laws do not apply beyond the Jews who want to keep practicing them, which freed Paul and the other apostles to welcome Gentiles to the family of God without forcing them to adopt Jewish culture.

Have traditions in your life become more important than biblical principles, without you realizing it? Have you been shaped by a religious culture that subtly or overtly excludes people from a different background or makes it difficult for them to draw near to Jesus in your context? Is God calling you to let go of certain religious traditions in your life? Is he calling you to declare certain things clean?

Reflect and Respond

What is Jesus saying to me right now?

What step of faith is Jesus calling me to take today?

DAY 27

READ AND LISTEN: MARK 7:24-37

Take a minute to listen for what the Spirit is saying in these verses...

COMMENT AND CONSIDER

After engaging in direct conflict with the religious teachers from Jerusalem and making such a radical declaration as to call all food ritually pure, Jesus departed from his mission field among the Jewish towns of upper Galilee and took his disciples to the coast of the Mediterranean north of Israel. We have seen how Jesus had a regular rhythm of rest and fruitful work on a daily and weekly basis, and following seasons of busy ministry. Now we see that occasionally Jesus took the disciples completely out of the area to a primarily Gentile region where they could unplug and rest in anonymity. This longer retreat was to the region of the large Gentile city of Tyre, located in modern-day Lebanon.

There is something truly refreshing about getting away from your familiar surroundings and going to a completely different cultural and geographical environment. Mark tells us specifically that Jesus and the disciples stayed in an extended family home where no one knew who they were. As a public person, it is difficult to really rest and relax when everywhere you go people recognize you and want to receive something from you. Jesus tried to create an environment of anonymity where they could find true rest and renewal.

In this context, a local woman recognized Jesus and approached him, asking him to come and deliver her demonized daughter. He replied, *"Let the children be fed first, because it isn't right to take the children's bread and throw it to the dogs."* In Middle Eastern culture, dogs are generally avoided because they are assumed to be feral and dangerous. First-century Jews often used the term *dog* as a derogatory reference to unclean Gentiles. Jesus' response seems surprisingly harsh, especially in light of his compassionate engagement with other Gentiles like the Gerasene demoniac (see Mark 5:1-20) and his recent abolishment of the judgmental divisions created by ritual purity laws.

It is true that Jesus told the disciples their missional focus would be *"the lost sheep of the house of Israel,"* by which he meant the Jewish peasants of upper Galilee. (Matthew 10:6) This was not to exclude the Gentiles, but to recognize the people of Israel as the starting point for the establishment of God's Kingdom. Paul had a similar priority in his mission, *"For I am not ashamed of the gospel, because it is the power of God for salvation to everyone who believes, first to the Jew, and also to the Greek."* (Romans 1:16) It is also helpful to remember Jesus took the disciples to Tyre specifically so they would not be recognized in order to find a much-needed time of deeper rest.

Despite Jesus' missional priorities and need for rest, this strong, clever, and faithful woman persisted in her entreaty. Instead of reacting defensively, she responded to Jesus' harsh statement by further developing the metaphor of the dog and children eating bread. Framing the dog as a beloved household pet rather than a dangerous feral animal, she said, *"Lord, even the dogs under the table eat the children's crumbs."* Notice the humility she adopted by calling Jesus *"Lord"* and accepting the depiction as a dog. Jesus was so moved by her humility and faith that he affirmed her and delivered her daughter from a distance. (See Matthew 15:28.) And then, as if to reinforce Jesus' compassion and welcome of Gentiles, Mark tells of Jesus' continued travels in the Gentile regions of Sidon and the Decapolis and the healing of a presumably Gentile deaf man there.

Who are you called to reach with the Good News? Are there rhythms you need to establish and boundaries you need to set to make opportunities for deeper rest and renewal?

Reflect and Respond

What is Jesus saying to me right now?

What step of faith is Jesus calling me to take today?

DAY 28

READ AND LISTEN: MARK 8:1-10
Take a minute to listen for what the Spirit is saying in these verses…

COMMENT AND CONSIDER

It was like déjà vu. This time Jesus had been teaching crowds of people for three days, and they had run out of food. As before, there was no easy way for them to buy more food, and Jesus asked the disciples how much food they had. They were only able to find seven loaves of bread and a few fish for the 4,000 people, so Jesus did it again. He gave thanks to God, broke the loaves and fish into 12 pieces, and gave them to the disciples to distribute. As before, the entire crowd ate their fill, and this time there were seven large baskets of leftovers. Another miracle!

Jesus' miraculous feeding of the 5,000 is recorded in all four Gospels, while only Matthew and Mark record the feeding of the 4,000. Matthew and Mark seem to place the feeding of the 5,000 on the west side of the lake, near Capernaum at Tabgha, while the feeding of the 4,000 is in *"a desolate place"* which seems to be on the east side of the lake. In both miraculous feedings, Jesus asked the disciples to provide the food, then showed them how to offer it up to the Father, and then had them distribute the food to the crowds. This means they were not only able to observe Jesus' example, but also participate in the miracle itself. Imagine wading into the crowd of 4,000 hungry people with a pitifully small amount of food and then watching it literally multiply in your very hands!

Discipleship is a relationship in which disciples learned to know what their rabbi knew and do what their rabbi did. This process began with disciples simply watching and listening to their rabbi. But as time went on, the rabbi began to invite his disciples to help him with more hands-on engagement. Eventually, the rabbi gave his disciples more and more responsibility, while still coaching them and offering constructive feedback, until finally the disciples were ready to strike out on their own, call disciples, and start the process all over again. This process could take from the age of 18 to 30 years old to complete.

Jesus took the Twelve disciples through this same process over the course of his time with them. But he did it in about three years rather than 12! His strategy was to give them full access to his life, investing everything he had in them while at the same time challenging them to do things far beyond their natural ability so they had to trust God's Spirit to guide and empower them. The result, at least for 11 of the 12, was that they learned to do the things Jesus did, including the supernatural things! Participating in the multiplication of loaves and fishes was part of this process of discipleship.

Too often we reduce discipleship to the transfer of information, as if we can become disciples simply by attending a class or reading a book or watching a video. Those can provide good information, but without a relationship in which we are close enough to someone who is ahead of us on the journey, we will not have a model to imitate. We also shy away from challenging each other as disciples and tend to over-emphasize providing resources. Jesus constantly gave the disciples insights, support, and training, but he was also bold to challenge the disciples to step out of their comfort zone and into dependence on the Holy Spirit. As a result, they came back from their first mission trip with testimonies of healing, deliverance, and changed lives!

Do you have someone in your life who is both inviting you close to invest in you and challenging you to step out of your comfort zone? Who are you investing in and challenging to follow Jesus more closely?

Reflect and Respond

What is Jesus saying to me right now?

What step of faith is Jesus calling me to take today?

DAY 29

READ AND LISTEN: MARK 8:11-21

Take a minute to listen for what the Spirit is saying in these verses...

COMMENT AND CONSIDER

It must have been frustrating to be Jesus! The incarnate second person of the Trinity who emptied himself and lived as a man in perfect union with the Father was not omniscient, but he walked in an incredible level of understanding and insight about the purposes of the Father. The depth of Jesus' teaching demonstrates his absolute brilliance, and the breadth of Jesus' power demonstrates his oneness with the Father's will. And yet so often people, even his closest disciples, did not understand Jesus. This time the Pharisees argued with him and demanded he perform a supernatural sign that would confirm the truth of his teaching and the validity of his authority.

A sign points us to something beyond itself. In the Gospel of John, seven of Jesus' miracles are described as *"signs"* that point to who Jesus is, the divine Son of God anointed as King to save his people and show us how we are meant to live. What more did the Pharisees need to believe Jesus is who he claimed to be? They had seen him make the lame walk and the blind see. They had watched him feed huge crowds with a handful of bread and fish. They heard testimony he had walked on water, calmed the stormy seas, and even raised a little girl from the dead!

Sometimes we see what we want to see and hear what we want to hear. Jesus knew no "sign" would satisfy the Pharisees' demand for verification, because they were not open to him. The word Mark uses in verse 12 to describe Jesus' reaction to this demand means "to groan inwardly." At a spiritual level, Jesus was deeply weary with the constant manipulation and opposition of these religious leaders to the Good News of the Kingdom. He knew there was no point in engaging their hardened hearts, so he simply told them *"no sign will be given,"* gathered his disciples, got in the boat, and sailed to the other side of the lake.

In the boat he tried to warn his disciples about the corrupting allure of political and religious power. *"Watch out! Beware of the leaven of the Pharisees and the leaven of Herod."* In the modern world we think of yeast in positive terms because it makes baked goods light and fluffy. In the ancient world, leaven was made by holding back part of the dough and letting it ferment so it released gas into the new dough and caused it to rise. It was always tricky to let the leaven ferment enough to release gas, but not so much that it turned bad and poisoned your family! This is why leaven was a common metaphor for how evil can spread and infect a group of people.

But once again, even his own disciples didn't understand Jesus. Because Jesus had just fed the four thousand, all they could think about was physical bread, and they assumed he was chiding them for forgetting to buy bread for the journey. He reminded them of the miraculous excess after everyone was full to explain it wasn't about the bread! Jesus was challenging them to open their eyes and ears, to listen more closely and tune their hearts to the word he was giving them.

Do you understand what Jesus is trying to tell you? Are your ears open to his word? Are your eyes open to his works? Is your heart receptive? Are you aware of the subtle influence that the kingdoms of this world can have on you?

REFLECT AND RESPOND
What is Jesus saying to me right now?

What step of faith is Jesus calling me to take today?

DAY 30

READ AND LISTEN: MARK 8:22-26
Take a minute to listen for what the Spirit is saying in these verses…

COMMENT AND CONSIDER
According to the Gospel accounts, Jesus spent a large amount of time and energy healing broken people. If we have not witnessed or experienced supernatural healing, it is easy to gloss over these passages and focus instead on his teaching and more comprehensible actions. But if we are disciples, we must take seriously the example Jesus has set for us. He said, *"Follow me,"* and that means we are to model our lives on his. Even if we feel uncomfortable about it, we cannot be Jesus' disciples and ignore his healing ministry.

Jesus healed people for two reasons. First, it was an expression of his love and compassion for all people. Love means acting in the best interests of others. Compassion means sharing the pain of those who are hurting. Jesus felt the pain of those who were hurting. Jesus loved broken people. So he did what he could to alleviate their pain and make them whole. Second, Jesus demonstrated the nature of God's Kingdom. In heaven there is no sickness, no suffering, no disease, and no injury. The Kingdom of God is defined by God's will being done on earth as it is done in heaven. That means when someone is healed, it is a demonstration that God's Kingdom is coming into our midst. (See Matthew 12:28.)

It is important to note Jesus is never recorded as praying to the Father and asking him to heal. Instead, Jesus acted as an authorized representative of his Father the King and confronted pain, sickness, and injury directly to heal. He rebuked the fever that plagued Simon's mother-in-law. (See Luke 4:39.) He commanded the skin disease to leave the leper, and it did. (See Mark 1:41.) He told the hemorrhaging woman *"be healed,"* and she was. (Mark 5:34)

So-called healers and exorcists in the first century typically employed esoteric spells and theatrical gestures while trying to affect a cure. Jesus, on the other hand, simply spoke authoritative words and people were healed. Jesus also used physical touch in his healings. He touched the eyes of the blind men in Jericho, and they were able to see. (Matthew 20:34.) Here in Bethsaida, we read that Jesus spit on the man's eyes and laid his hands on him. It was as if Jesus purposely said and did something different almost every time he healed to make it clear there was no magical formula. Instead, he showed us it is all about exercising God's authority by faith.

When Jesus healed the blind man in Bethsaida, he asked him to test out his eyes. As the man opened his eyes he reported, *"I see people—they look like trees walking."* He was experiencing a partial healing, so Jesus pressed in and placed his hands on the man's eyes again. Then the man's sight was fully restored. This is a reminder that healing ministry is a kind of spiritual warfare. We do not have to try and convince our heavenly Father to heal. He loves his children and wants us to be whole and well. The challenge is to overcome the brokenness of this fallen world and the enemy of our soul who wants to steal, kill, and destroy everything that is good. This means we have to fight by faith to overcome the roadblocks that are preventing the power of God from healing.

Jesus gave his disciples authority and power to heal in his name. He has given us that same authority and power. The question is whether we will learn how to use it to show compassion and to demonstrate the Kingdom. Do you believe God's power can flow through you to do his will on earth as it is done in heaven? Do you care about the hurting enough to engage in healing ministry the way Jesus did?

REFLECT AND RESPOND

What is Jesus saying to me right now?

What step of faith is Jesus calling me to take today?

Footsteps Every Week: Review

Write a brief summary of what Jesus said to you each day this past week and the step of faith he called you to take:

Monday

Tuesday

Wednesday

Thursday

Friday

Saturday

Footsteps Every Week: Reflect

Big Picture
As you look over what Jesus has said to you this past week, do you see any themes? What is the most important thing you need to remember and believe?

Predictable Pattern
As you look over what Jesus called you to do this past week, is there a new predictable pattern he is inviting you to establish in your life with God and others?

Plant the Word
As you look over the readings from this past week, write out the passage that feels most important for you and memorize it over the next week:

DAY 31

READ AND LISTEN: MARK 8:27-9:1

Take a minute to listen for what the Spirit is saying in these verses...

COMMENT AND CONSIDER

Jesus took the disciples to the far north of Israel, to the Greek city called Caesarea Philippi, a site infamous for the worship of the god Pan. Near the pagan temples built around the Cave of Pan was a powerful waterfall that still fills a beautiful gorge with cooling mist. This seems to be the area Jesus took his disciples for a time of rest and refreshment. On the way Jesus engaged them in rabbinical dialogue. Often rabbis taught by asking questions and then commenting on the answers given by their disciples. Jesus asked them about the various rumors swirling around about his identity, *"Who do people say that I am?"* After they commented on the different ideas about him, Jesus made it more personal, *"But you, who do you say that I am?"* Peter spoke up and said, *"You are the Messiah."*

The Hebrew word *"Messiah"* literally means "anointed one." The ancient kings of Israel were traditionally anointed at their coronation. Ever since the time of King David, the people of Israel had waited for God to fulfill his promise that he would raise up a descendant of David to be the anointed King to save God's people and establish a kingdom that would go on forever. (See 2 Samuel 7:11-13.) Most Jews assumed this "Anointed One" (Greek: "Christ") would come as a military ruler to overthrow the Romans and establish an earthly kingdom of justice. Some, reading Daniel 7:13-14, believed the Messiah would be *"one like a son of man"* who descended from heaven as a divine warrior of God to defeat Israel's enemies.

Jesus affirmed Peter's profession of faith in him as Messiah but went on to define what kind of Messiah he would be. *"He began to teach them that it was necessary for the Son of Man to suffer many things and be rejected by the elders, chief priests, and scribes, be killed, and rise after three days."* Peter voiced the horror they all felt at these words by rebuking his master, but Jesus responded, *"Get *behind me, Satan! You are not thinking about God's concerns but human concerns."* We all want a Messiah who fits our own expectations. We want God to save us, but we want him to do it our way. Peter wanted a Messiah who would storm Jerusalem, kick the Roman legions out of the Antonia Fortress, and take up residence in Herod's Palace. None of them could fathom a Messiah who would willingly lay down his life, but that is exactly the kind of King Jesus came to be.

Had Jesus organized a military rebellion and overthrown the Roman military might, he could have established an earthly kingdom. But that kingdom, like all that had come before it, would not last. His rule is based on a power greater than any other power on earth, the power of self-giving love. This kind of love captures the human heart and transforms the whole person. He knew the only way to accomplish that was to submit to the forces of darkness that would eventually nail him to a cross. This is where King Jesus is enthroned, on the hearts of those who receive and follow him to the cross. This is how the Kingdom of God comes, through the life of every disciple who is filled with the Holy Spirit and following the example of Jesus by taking up their cross and laying down their life in love.

Are you trying to make Jesus into the kind of Messiah you want him to be, or are you laying down your life by following Jesus as your true King?

Reflect and Respond
What is Jesus saying to me right now?

What step of faith is Jesus calling me to take today?

DAY 32

READ AND LISTEN: MARK 9:2-13

Take a minute to listen for what God is saying in these verses…

COMMENT AND CONSIDER

Jesus took his three closest disciples up a *"high mountain."* The traditional location for Jesus' transfiguration is on top of Mount Tabor (1,843 feet), a loaf-shaped mountain in the Jezreel Valley just southeast of Nazareth. However, a Roman camp stood at the top of that mountain in the first century, and Jesus and the disciples were on retreat at the foot of the much higher Mount Hermon (9,166 feet elevation). So it is more likely Mount Hermon that they climbed that day. While on the mountain, Jesus was *"transfigured"* (Greek: *metamorpho*), meaning his appearance was dramatically changed before the disciples' very eyes. Mark describes a kind of supernatural light emanating from Jesus and shining out through his clothes.

When Moses went up on Mount Sinai, his face took on radiant glow, reflecting the glory of the God he encountered there. Elijah was taken up into heaven on a fiery chariot pulled by horses of fire, reflective of the glory into which he was ascending. Now Jesus shined with that same divine glory, except it came from within him, not as a reflection. Although Deuteronomy 34:6 records the burial of Moses, it states that the location of his grave was unknown. This led some rabbis to conclude that Moses had also ascended into heaven without dying like Elijah. And so, it was perhaps not totally surprising that these two figures of radiant glory appeared with Jesus in the glow of his divine glory!

Both Moses and Elijah suffered because of their faithful obedience and were rejected by the people of Israel, but ultimately vindicated by God. This is exactly what was happening to Jesus. Furthermore, people were waiting for the "Prophet like Moses" to liberate them from slavery once and for all. (See Deuteronomy 18:15.) The prophet Malachi foretold that Elijah was going to return from heaven before the great and glorious day of the Lord.

(See Malachi 4:5-6.) Their presence with Jesus in this moment of divine revelation confirmed Jesus' role as the Messianic Redeemer who came to set God's people free.

As if all this were not enough, a voice from heaven made it unmistakably clear what it meant: *"This is my beloved Son; listen to him!"* Although the Second Person of the Trinity had emptied himself, taken on the limitations of full humanity, and functioned on earth as a human being just like us, he did not forfeit his full divinity. This was one of those moments when the fulness of Jesus' divine nature broke through the limitations of his earthly body and the glory of his divinity could no longer be contained.

Mark reports that the disciples were terrified by this display of supernatural glory, but Peter spoke up anyway and lamely suggested building some temporary shelters for the three of them, perhaps reflecting the familiar practice of building "booths" on top of their houses during the festival. It may be that they were terrified that the glory of God would overpower them and even kill them, so Peter could have been suggesting the booths as a kind of veil that would protect them from exposure to too much glory.

On the way down the mountain, the disciples asked Jesus about the prophecy that Elijah would return before the Messiah comes. Jesus responded, *"Elijah has come, and they did whatever they pleased to him,"* pointing to John the Baptist as the fulfillment of the prophecy.

The transfiguration is one of the clearest revelations in the dual nature of Jesus, that he was both fully human and fully divine. When you look at Jesus which of his natures stands out the most to you? What is helpful about seeing Jesus' full humanity? What is helpful about recognizing his full divinity?

REFLECT AND RESPOND

What is Jesus saying to me right now?

What step of faith is Jesus calling me to take today?

DAY 33

READ AND LISTEN: MARK 9:14-29
Take a minute to listen for what the Spirit is saying in these verses…

COMMENT AND CONSIDER
As Jesus, Peter, James, and John came down from the mountain, they found the rest of the disciples embroiled in a controversy. A man had brought his son who seemed to be suffering from some kind of demonic epilepsy, but the disciples were unable to deliver and heal him. This gave the religious leaders an opening to attack the disciples, and everyone was in an uproar when Jesus and the other disciples arrived.

In the ancient world, people tended to attribute powers they could not explain to unclean spirits and demons. In the modern western world, we tend to assume every phenomenon has a rational, scientific explanation. But the truth is more complicated than either worldview recognizes. Jesus often addressed people's physical infirmities and healed them with supernatural power. He also addressed people's spiritual condition and delivered people from demonization and spiritual oppression. Sometimes these two kinds of conditions are mixed up together, as they seemed to be for the son of this desperate father.

Since childhood the boy had suffered from what sounds like epileptic seizures and was unable to speak, but Jesus discerned a spiritual cause as well. Clearly at his wit's end, the father asked Jesus, *"But if you can do anything, have compassion on us and help us."* Jesus replied, *"'If you can'? Everything is possible for the one who believes."* Jesus was pointing out that faith is the key to healing and deliverance. The word translated *"believes"* here is the verbal form of the word for "faith." It literally means to put faith into action. After healing people Jesus often pointed to the faith of the person who was healed as the key to their healing. (See Matthew 9:22; Mark 10:52; etc.) Mark tells us Jesus could not do many miracles in Nazareth because of their refusal to believe. (See Mark 6:5-6.)

This father offered a remarkable cry in reply to Jesus' challenge: *"I do believe; help my unbelief!"* What an accurate description of our human condition. We are all a mixture of faith and doubt. But this man refused to let his doubts define him. Instead, he chose to express the faith Jesus' words had planted in his heart. As Paul says, *"So faith comes from hearing, and what is heard comes through the word of Christ."* (Romans 10:17) He heard Jesus' promise and that gave him at least a tiny bit of faith. Jesus said, *"For truly I tell you, if you have faith the size of a mustard seed, you will tell this mountain, 'Move from here to there,' and it will move. Nothing will be impossible for you."* (Matthew 17:20)

This man is an example for all of us who are facing insurmountable obstacles. He cried out to Jesus and listened to his promise. Even if his doubts towered above him, he took the mustard seed of faith Jesus planted in his heart and exercised it. And it was enough to save his son!

Afterward the disciples asked Jesus privately why they were not able to liberate the boy, and Jesus pointed them to a deeper connection with God through prayer. They did not need to learn some special form of prayer to heal the boy; they needed to learn a greater submission to and dependence on their Father, so his power could flow through them more effectively by faith. It is not about who is doing the healing. It is not about a certain technique or mysterious incantations. It is about exercising faith in the authority given to us by our Father the King to do his will on earth as it is done in heaven.

What do you need to trust God for today? Are you listening for Jesus' faith-producing word to you? Are you exercising the mustard seed of faith he is giving you?

Reflect and Respond

What is Jesus saying to me right now?

What step of faith is Jesus calling me to take today?

DAY 34

READ AND LISTEN: MARK 9:30-37
Take a minute to listen for what the Spirit is saying in these verses…

COMMENT AND CONSIDER
From almost the beginning of Jesus' public mission the religious and political leaders were threatened by his authority and power. It was not long before they were intentionally plotting to silence Jesus once and for all. As Jesus' popularity swelled and the nature of his messianic claims began to circulate, the tensions grew. Jesus often told people he healed or delivered not to tell anyone because he was trying to keep this conflict with the religious leaders from spiraling out of control before he could complete his mission. Now Jesus' awareness of his ultimate destiny in Jerusalem was becoming more acute.

One of the reasons Jesus started spending more time in the Gentile areas was to avoid the religious and political leaders plotting against him. That is why Jesus traveled incognito and kept out of sight when he returned to Capernaum, his adopted hometown in Galilee. This was the second recorded prediction Jesus gave the disciples of his death and resurrection, but somehow, they couldn't seem to comprehend something so far outside of their expectations. By their frivolous arguments, the disciples demonstrated just how oblivious they were to the ominous events looming in their near future. Although they were embarrassed to admit they had been arguing about who would have top ranking in the administration of Jesus' new government, he knew it anyway.

Jesus gave them a very different definition of greatness in his Kingdom when he said, *"If anyone wants to be first, he must be last and servant of all."* And then he scooped up a little child into his arms. In the ancient world where nearly half of all children died before the age of 12, they were not generally considered valuable until they had proven their longevity and usefulness. It was the physically strong, powerful, wealthy, and those of high social rank that were considered great. The little child in Jesus' arms was none of those things. And yet Jesus lifted her up as a model of greatness.

Jesus could easily have leveraged his power and fame to serve his own status, but he consistently did the opposite. Instead of using his position to consolidate his own power by making others dependent on him, Jesus gave his power away. From the beginning he trained and empowered his disciples to do everything he did. His plan was to invest himself in his disciples in such a way that, within three years, they would no longer need him to show them the way, but they could do the same with others. This culture of selfless leadership, focused on raising up and empowering disciples, is what caused the movement of Jesus to spread so powerfully across the Roman empire that in less than three centuries a majority of Romans had become followers of Jesus!

Jesus gave his disciples a profoundly counter-cultural way of looking at others. Rather than waiting to see if they became strong enough to do something for them, Jesus taught his disciples to welcome and invest in those who were younger and were considered insignificant because they had little to offer. This meant laying down their lives and functioning as servants, rather than seeking position and prestige to build their power and influence. But Jesus showed them that, paradoxically, this is precisely the path to greatness in his Kingdom.

What are the marks of greatness in the kingdoms of your world? How does true greatness in the Kingdom of God differ from that? What can you do today to live as a servant of all by investing in those who have nothing to offer in return?

Reflect and Respond
What is Jesus saying to me right now?

What step of faith is Jesus calling me to take today?

DAY 35

READ AND LISTEN: MARK 9:38-50
Take a minute to listen for what the Spirit is saying in these verses…

COMMENT AND CONSIDER
When we receive something especially valuable or meaningful it is natural to guard it closely because we are afraid of losing it. The disciples realized what a unique honor it was to live in such close relationship with Jesus, but along with the sense of honor, a feeling of entitlement started to creep in. Being part of the inner circle made them feel as if they had special rights to represent Jesus. When they saw someone else carrying out the same deliverance ministry Jesus had trained them to do, their sense of privilege was threatened.

When they told Jesus about this rogue exorcist, he told them not to interfere. *"Don't stop him, because there is no one who will perform a miracle in my name who can soon afterward speak evil of me. For whoever is not against us is for us."* We don't know how this man came to follow Jesus, but it is clear he was a disciple who represented Jesus and followed his example by exercising power in love. On another occasion Jesus said, *"I have other sheep that are not from this sheep pen; I must bring them also, and they will listen to my voice."* (John 10:16) This man was one of those *"other sheep."*

Jesus' Kingdom is inclusive not elitist. There is room for everyone who will say yes to Jesus. Leadership in that Kingdom is for every person who will submit to Jesus and follow him. Although this man was not following the disciples, he was following the example of Jesus. He was rightly representing Jesus and doing God's will on earth as it is in heaven. We should never be threatened when we see others doing great things in Jesus' name, only encouraged. Even a cup of cold water is a sign that someone is with us, not against us. There is no room for competition or jealousy in the Kingdom of God. We are all part of the same family.

Of course, this is a different situation than the case of Simon the magician in Samaria who thought he could buy spiritual authority and power from the apostles. (See Acts 8:14-25.) Or the case of the sons of Sceva in Ephesus, who didn't know Jesus but tried to exercise power in his name. (See Acts 19:11-20.) These are examples of spiritual counterfeits trying to co-opt Jesus' power for their own ends. This kind of spiritual manipulation and abuse is never to be tolerated. When the religious leaders accused Jesus of being empowered by demons, he said, *"Anyone who is not with me is against me."* (Matthew 12:30)

In Capernaum still today, we see the huge olive crushing stones that were turned in a round base by donkeys in Jesus' time. Jesus warned those spiritual manipulators who would harm *"these little ones who believe in me"* that it would be better for them if one of these huge millstones were tied around their neck and they were thrown into the lake! He used the human body as an illustration of how to deal with such people. *"And if your hand causes you to fall away, cut it off... if your foot causes you to fall away, cut it off... if your eye causes you to fall away, gouge it out."*

As welcoming and inclusive as God's Kingdom is, we also need to protect our spiritual family by removing those who prove to be predators. Who do you need to welcome and affirm, even if they make you feel threatened? Who do you need to distance from your community to protect the vulnerable people in your midst?

Reflect and Respond

What is Jesus saying to me right now?

What step of faith is Jesus calling me to take today?

DAY 36

READ AND LISTEN: MARK 10:1-12

Take a minute to listen for what the Spirit is saying in these verses...

COMMENT AND CONSIDER

When God created the Universe, he formed man and woman *"in his own image."* (Genesis 1:26-27) This means they had the same relationship to God as biological children who bear a resemblance to their parents. We are the beloved children of God! The man and woman were also given the authority to *"rule"* over all of creation on behalf of God. (See Genesis 1:26-28) This means they were commissioned to carry out God's will on earth as it is in heaven. We are authorized representatives of our Father the King! Part of this good design is a partnership of oneness between a man and a woman meant to multiply God's goodness by creating a lifelong indivisible partnership of oneness between them. *"Be fruitful, multiply."* (Genesis 1:28)

The oneness of marriage is meant to provide a stable, loving environment for children to grow into the multiplication of fruitfulness in their own lives. However, Adam and Eve made a fateful choice when they decided they didn't need to rule on God's behalf but could rule their lives and creation independently of God. The result was a terrible fracture in relationships. The man and woman were ashamed and separated from their Father the King. Eventually this relational brokenness crept into marriage, and divorce began to shatter the union that was meant to nurture the multiplication of goodness.

The Old Testament Law recognized divorce as a given reality in a broken world, neither affirming nor forbidding it. But it did require a man to write a certificate of record when divorcing his wife so she could prove her single status and be eligible for marriage. They typically read, "Lo, thou art free to marry any man." This record was critical for her survival in a world where unmarried female independence was limited to prostitutes and beggars.

By the time of Jesus, it was very easy for a man to divorce his wife. The first century Jewish historian Josephus wrote he divorced his second wife simply because he was "displeased with her behavior." Based on Proverbs 18:22, one rabbi even claimed it was virtuous to divorce a "bad" wife! Jewish law did not allow a wife to divorce her husband without his consent, although this was possible in the Greco-Roman world. There were instances of aristocratic Jewish women unilaterally divorcing their husbands in the first century, but usually they were functioning in a Roman legal context.

As Jesus drew near to Jerusalem, some Pharisees questioned him about the legality of divorce. Jesus conceded that Moses allowed a man to divorce his wife with a certificate but pointed out this was a concession to human sinfulness. Jesus made it clear this was not God's design for marriage. The Kingdom Jesus proclaimed is about doing God's will on earth as it is done in heaven. There is no divorce in heaven, so there is no divorce in the Kingdom. Jesus summed it up by saying, *"Therefore what God has joined together, let no one separate."* When his disciples questioned him privately about this, Jesus took it a step further, saying remarriage after divorce was a kind of adultery, because the original union is meant to be lifelong.

This was a challenging teaching in the first century and even more in our time when the divorce rate is over 50% and nearly 80% of divorced people remarry. Jesus cast an inspiring vision for the Kingdom of God with incredibly high moral standards. (See Matthew 5:17-48.) But he also built a spiritual family with an incredibly gracious welcome. (See Mark 2:16-17.) What does it mean for you to hold these two realities in tension? How can you be as morally uncompromising and as relationally gracious as Jesus?

Reflect and Respond
What is Jesus saying to me right now?

What step of faith is Jesus calling me to take today?

Footsteps Every Week: Review

Write a brief summary of what Jesus said to you each day this past week and the step of faith he called you to take:

Monday

Tuesday

Wednesday

Thursday

Friday

Saturday

Footsteps Every Week: Reflect

Big Picture
As you look over what Jesus has said to you this past week, do you see any themes? What is the most important thing you need to remember and believe?

Predictable Pattern
As you look over what Jesus called you to do this past week, is there a new predictable pattern he is inviting you to establish in your life with God and others?

Plant the Word
As you look over the readings from this past week, write out the passage that feels most important for you and memorize it over the next week:

DAY 37

READ AND LISTEN: MARK 10:13-16

Take a minute to listen for what the Spirit is saying in these verses…

COMMENT AND CONSIDER

As we have seen, the ancient world was a dangerous place for children. Sources indicate that six out of ten children died before the age of 16. That means in a family with five children, on average only two would make it to adulthood. This resulted in a high level of parental anxiety, especially in a child's younger and more vulnerable years. It also caused parents to keep emotional distance from their children until they became more viable. Imagine a mother who had already lost two or three children, holding a new baby in her arms. It would be very difficult to expose yourself to more grief by bonding with a child that you knew might soon die.

So with Jesus' reputation as a powerful healer and exorcist, it is not surprising that parents brought their little children to Jesus in the hope that he would touch their child and ward off evil spirits and anything else that would threaten their lives. We have read over and over again about the aggressive crowds that chased Jesus and the disciples around the lake to their place of retreat, surrounded them, pressed in to try and touch Jesus, and at times threatened to overwhelm them. It is also not surprising the disciples would become protective of Jesus, concerned for his safety, and even weary and calloused to those who were trying to get close to their rabbi.

For all these reasons, the disciples tried to prevent these fearful parents from pressing their children into Jesus' arms. Perhaps the *"rebuke"* Mark records was the disciples shouting at these anxious parents to take their children and go away. When Jesus realized what was happening, he was indignant with his disciples. He showed them the Kingdom of God operates on a different set of values than the kingdoms of this world when he said, *"Let the little children come to me. Don't stop them, because the kingdom of God belongs to such as these."* This was a radically counter-cultural thing to say in a world where children had no power, status, or rights. The rabbis categorized children with the deaf, the mute, the weak-minded, and slaves. Children were not considered full persons and were treated more like property than human beings.

Jesus not only described the Kingdom of God; he also demonstrated it. To show them how things work in the Kingdom, Jesus motioned to these children to come to him. As they ran to him and surrounded him, he began hugging them, laying his hands on them, and speaking over them words affirming their true value as beloved children of God. In a world where children were invisible and insignificant, Jesus demonstrated their true value and worth as the heavenly Father's image-bearers.

Jesus took it one step further when he turned to his disciples and told them, *"Truly I tell you, whoever does not receive the kingdom of God like a little child will never enter it."* Not only are little children accepted in God's Kingdom; they are the role models for all who would seek to join them! Jesus tells us humility is a prerequisite to living in God's Kingdom. The Kingdom is the reality we experience when we are fully surrendered to God's reign in our lives. That means recognizing we are not in charge; we are not in control. It means submitting ourselves to the true King and giving his Spirit the freedom to reign in and through us.

Who do you look down on as less than you? How does Jesus' vision of the Kingdom reframe those value judgments? What does it mean for you to humble yourself as a little child in order to enter more fully into the Kingdom of God?

Reflect and Respond
What is Jesus saying to me right now?

What step of faith is Jesus calling me to take today?

DAY 38

READ AND LISTEN: MARK 10:17-22
Take a minute to listen for what the Spirit is saying in these verses...

COMMENT AND CONSIDER
A man who seemed to have it all ran up and knelt before Jesus. Matthew tells us he was a young man, Luke tells us he was a ruler, and they all confirm he was very rich. (See Matthew 19:22 and Luke 18:18.) He could have been one of the local synagogue rulers or a city official working under Herod Antipas. It is not surprising that he is rich, for positions of authority were often connected to wealth. But it is unusual for someone to have this level of social status at a young age.

In addressing Jesus as a *"good teacher"* and asking how to inherit eternal life, this man revealed something about his worldview. In ancient Judaism wealth was often assumed to be a sign of God's blessing. It would be easy for this man to assume what many others did—that his wealth proved he was a good man living a good life. By applying the adjective *"good"* to Jesus' title *"teacher,"* this man also assumed Jesus' position was the basis of his goodness. Jesus' response to this man's greeting was not a rejection of the assessment he was good, but rather a challenge of this man's definition of goodness.

The man's question further reinforced his skewed understanding of goodness. His assumption was salvation is something that must be earned by obedience; that there is something he *must do* to inherit eternal life. When Jesus lists four of the ten commandments, the young man replies, *"Teacher, I have kept all these from my youth."* Jesus taught that murder includes speaking unkindly to someone, and adultery includes looking on someone with lust in your heart. It is highly unlikely this man had kept the Law at this level of purity. As Jesus said, the demand of the Law is to *"be perfect, therefore, as your heavenly Father is perfect."* (Matthew 5:48)

Instead, Jesus pointed this man to the source of true goodness by saying, *"No one is good except God alone."* Goodness is not something we can manufacture by our own religious rituals or moral efforts. God is good, and all goodness comes from God. The only way to become truly good in a broken world beset by evil is to be connected to the Source of true goodness. On another occasion a scribe asked Jesus the exact same question: *"What must I do to inherit eternal life?"* Jesus pointed him to the two great commandments, *"love the Lord your God"* and *"love your neighbor."* (Luke 10:25-28) It is only by living in an intimate and loving relationship with God that we become truly good and are able to do truly good things, like loving our neighbor.

As Jesus interacted with this man, he recognized the thing standing in his way of entering a transformative relationship with God were his possessions. There was no judgment on Jesus' part; he simply looked at him and loved him. But Jesus loved him too much to leave him trapped by his possessions, so he gave this man the hard truth. *"You lack one thing: Go, sell all you have and give to the poor, and you will have treasure in heaven. Then come, follow me."* In one of the most tragic moments recorded in the Gospels, this man was unwilling to let go of that which had such a grip on his soul. Rather than sell everything to buy the field with the priceless buried treasure, he traded his priceless birthright for worthless trinkets.

How do you define goodness in your life? How can you allow God's goodness to shape your life more fully? What is something Jesus is calling you to let go of so you can follow him more closely?

Reflect and Respond

What is Jesus saying to me right now?

What step of faith is Jesus calling me to take today?

DAY 39

READ AND LISTEN: MARK 10:23-31
Take a minute to listen for what the Spirit is saying in these verses…

COMMENT AND CONSIDER
As the disciples watched the rich young ruler walk away, perhaps they thought about what a good addition he would have been to their group. He sure seemed like a more upstanding citizen than Matthew the tax collector or Simon the Zealot! Judas must have pondered how much he could have added to their operating budget. Maybe they wondered why Jesus didn't soften the challenge a bit. How about give away *some* of your possessions and come follow me? The rabbis said 20% was the most someone should give to the poor lest they become poor themselves. But Jesus knew it would take a completely new financial start for this man to be free of all the ways money stood between him and the Kingdom of God.

Jesus began to process what happened with his disciples by saying, *"How hard it is for those who have wealth to enter the kingdom of God!"* This was a shocking thing for Jesus to say because wealth was seen as a sign of God's blessing. Everyone assumed the more money you had, the more God approved of you. How could wealth be an impediment to living under the reign of God? Jesus gave them a vivid picture of just how hard it is, *"It is easier for a camel to go through the eye of a needle than for a rich person to enter the kingdom of God."*

Various interpretations have been suggested to soften this statement, but it is clear both the disciples and Jesus understood it as a face-value metaphor for something impossible. It was as difficult for a rich person to enter the Kingdom of God as it was to fit the largest land mammal in Palestine through the tiniest opening in a typical household. Wealth is a powerful competitor for first place in the hearts and lives of those who possess it. The accumulation, management, and protection of wealth can take up a lot of time and energy, easily evolving into an obsession.

This wasn't the only time Jesus addressed the snares of money. In his parable of the sower, Jesus described the seed that falls among thorns, sprouts and grows, but ultimately gets chocked out by *"the deceitfulness of wealth."* (See Matthew 13:7, 22.) He also told the parable of the rich man who obsessively kept building bigger barns to store his accumulated wealth and then suddenly died and had to give an account for his life. (See Luke 12:16-21.) In his parable of the rich man and Lazarus, the stingy rich man ends up in torment in Hades, and Abraham tells him of the futility of warning his wealthy brothers. (See Luke 16:19-31.)

The disciples expressed their astonishment over Jesus' statement by asking, *"Then who can be saved?"* Jesus responded with the promise, *"With man this is impossible, but not with God, because all things are possible with God."* The point is rich and poor alike are only saved by grace. But Peter pressed in on the question of possessions by pointing out, *"Look, we have left everything and followed you."* His implied question is, "When we do give it all away, what will be left for us?" Jesus explained the paradoxical economy of the Kingdom by promising, *"Truly I tell you, there is no one who has left house or brothers or sisters or mother or father or children or fields for my sake and for the sake of the gospel, who will not receive a hundred times more, now at this time… and eternal life in the age to come."* If only the rich young ruler had understood how, in the Kingdom of God, giving everything away is how you get more than you could have imagined, now and in the world to come.

Are your possessions standing between you and the Kingdom of God in any way? Are there things you could give up to receive more of what God wants to give you now and in the life to come?

Reflect and Respond

What is Jesus saying to me right now?

What step of faith is Jesus calling me to take today?

DAY 40

READ AND LISTEN: MARK 10:32-45
Take a minute to listen for what the Spirit is saying in these verses…

COMMENT AND CONSIDER
Jesus and the disciples continued their journey toward Jerusalem, aiming to arrive in time to celebrate the Passover there. Mark's narrative is a reminder that Jesus did not travel with the twelve disciples exclusively. They were his full-time apprentices, but other disciples left home to travel with Jesus from time to time as well, including women disciples, a feature unique to Jesus among Jewish rabbis. (See Luke 8:1-3.) This is what Mark means when he says the twelve disciples were *"astonished,"* but the wider group of disciples were *"afraid."*

Each step along the road brought them closer to the holy city and heightened the sense of anticipation of what awaited them there. For the third time, Jesus pulled aside his closest twelve disciples and prophesied in even greater detail the fate that awaited him in Jerusalem. *"The Son of Man will be handed over to the chief priests and the scribes, and they will condemn him to death. Then they will hand him over to the Gentiles, and they will mock him, spit on him, flog him, and kill him, and he will rise after three days."*

It seems impossible the disciples could fail to understand what Jesus had told them, but the sons of Zebedee were still stuck on their assumption that the Messiah was a military leader who would rout the Romans and set up a new administration in the palace of Herod. Nothing could be further from the truth, as Jesus repeatedly made clear. Despite this clarity, James and John approached Jesus and asked, *"Allow us to sit at your right and at your left in your glory."* Roman Emperors sometimes sat their victorious generals on either side of their royal throne. This is the honor for which the *"Sons of Thunder"* seem to be asking. (Mark 3:17)

Jesus asked them if they really understood what it meant to sit at his side when he was establishing his Kingdom. They insisted they did, and Jesus gave them the ominous promise, *"You will drink the cup I drink, and you will be baptized with the baptism I am baptized with. But to sit at my right or left is not mine to give; instead, it is for those for whom it has been prepared."* They would share in Jesus' suffering. John would be the sole male disciple to stand at the foot of the cross and would eventually face exile on Patmos. (See John 19:25-27.) James would be the first of the twelve to face martyrdom at the edge of Herod Agrippa's sword. (See Acts 12:1-2.)

The Roman Empire was organized hierarchically with different levels of honor, privilege, and power, from Caesar and the Roman Senate at the top down to the peasants and slaves at the bottom. Jesus told the disciples this is not how they were to operate. Instead, he said they were to lead by serving. Greatness would be measured by humility. Those who end up sitting at Jesus' right and left hand are the ones willing to serve as he did. Jesus pointed to his own example as the model for leadership in the Kingdom of God, *"For even the Son of Man did not come to be served, but to serve, and to give his life as a ransom for many."*

Jesus willingly offered up his life as a sacrifice for the redemption of all humanity. While our calling is not as broad in scope, as disciples we are called to take up our cross and make the loving sacrifice of serving others. How is Jesus calling you to lay down your life? Who is God calling you to serve?

Reflect and Respond

What is Jesus saying to me right now?

What step of faith is Jesus calling me to take today?

DAY 41

READ AND LISTEN: MARK 10:46-52
Take a minute to listen for what the Spirit is saying in these verses…

COMMENT AND CONSIDER
A well-established pilgrim route led south from Galilee, along the eastern bank of the Jordan River, turned west to cross the river at the place where Jesus was baptized, passed through the ancient city of Jericho, then rose up the steep, winding route to the Mount of Olives and the city of Jerusalem. As the Passover drew nearer, the traffic on this road steadily increased until a constant flow of travelers passed through on their way to the Holy City. A blind man from Jericho shrewdly found a spot along that route so he could take advantage of the pilgrim practice of almsgiving.

Any time a minor character in the Gospels is named, it is a clue that this was one of the eyewitnesses who was part of the community for whom the Gospel was written. This was a way of confirming the accuracy of the apostolic account and affirming the presence of that person in the assembly of disciples. Tradition says Mark was Peter's disciple in Rome and took notes while listening to the Apostle's preaching. This is the only Gospel that names the blind beggar from Jericho, which probably means Bartimaeus, son of Timaeus, was sitting there in the group when Peter told this story, and the Apostle pointed to him and called out his name. Little details, like Mark's description of him throwing aside his cloak (probably laid before him to collect coins), add an element of authenticity which would only come from the memory of someone who was actually there—perhaps even from Bartimaeus himself!

That day in Jericho, Bartimaeus could tell something was happening by the sound of the crowd gathering in anticipation of Jesus' arrival. When someone saw Jesus coming, Bart began to yell over the crowd, *"Jesus, Son of David, have mercy on me!"* This was a particularly messianic title, highlighting God's promise to raise a descendant of David to be the king who would liberate the people of God and establish an eternal kingdom. Many rumors floated around about who this builder-turned-rabbi from nowheresville Nazareth might be, but Bartimaeus seemed sure he was the Messiah. Those standing around the blind man tried to quiet him down, embarrassed by his bold, presumptuous demands, but their scolding only made him yell louder.

Jesus heard the commotion and called for them to bring the blind man to him. When Jesus asked what he wanted, Bartimaeus answered, *"Rabboni, I want to see."* This Aramaic form of the word for rabbi means *"my teacher"* and is the language of a disciple speaking to his own rabbi. Jesus responded, *"Go, your faith has saved you,"* and immediately Bartimaeus' eyes were opened and he could see! Instead of going home, he began to follow Jesus and the other disciples on the road to Jerusalem.

When Jesus announced his mission in Nazareth, he quoted Isaiah 61 which says the Messiah will give *"recovery of sight to the blind."* (Luke 4:18) Isaiah also prophesied that when the Messiah came, the desert wilderness would begin to bloom like a garden and then said *"the eyes of the blind shall be opened, and the ears of the deaf shall be unstopped. Then shall the lame man leap as a hart, and the tongue of the dumb sing."* (Isaiah 35:5-6) There, in the desert oasis of Jericho, a blind man who could see that Jesus was the Messiah fulfilled this ancient prophecy!

What is keeping you from seeing Jesus more clearly? Are you willing to be as bold and presumptuous as Bartimaeus? What would you say to Jesus if he asked you, *"What do you want me to do for you?"*

REFLECT AND RESPOND
What is Jesus saying to me right now?

What step of faith is Jesus calling me to take today?

DAY 42

READ AND LISTEN: MARK 11:1-11
Take a minute to listen for what the Spirit is saying in these verses…

COMMENT AND CONSIDER
Jesus and his group of disciples departed Jericho and began the arduous day-long journey on the Ascent of Adummim (literally: "red ascent"), which climbs some 3,500 feet through the reddish sandstone of the desert hills and valleys up to Jerusalem. Its name was both a geographical reference and a reminder of the bloody bandits who attacked unwary travelers in this remote region. (See Luke 10:25-37.)

Coming to the southeastern slope of the Mount of Olives, they arrived at the village of Bethany where they stayed with the extended family of Mary, Martha, and Lazarus. In as much as Simon's extended family was Jesus' Galilean base, this family's home was Jesus' Jerusalem base. The next afternoon Jesus and the disciples set out on the final leg of their journey, a short 1.75-mile walk over the Mount of Olives, down through the Kidron Valley, and up into Jerusalem. The roads were filled with pilgrims waving palm branches and singing the Hallel Psalms (Psalm 113-118) in eager anticipation of their imminent entrance into the Holy City.

Jesus chose a specific way to enter Jerusalem that day. He sent two of his disciples to a nearby village to pick up a young donkey he had arranged ahead of time, and then rode the colt over the Mount of Olives. The Prophet Zechariah foretold the Messiah would appear dramatically on the Mount of Olives. (See Zechariah 14:4.) He also prophesied, *"Rejoice greatly, Daughter Zion! Shout in triumph, Daughter Jerusalem! Look, your King is coming to you; he is righteous and victorious, humble and riding on a donkey, on a colt, the foal of a donkey."* (Zechariah 9:9)

Jesus intentionally fulfilled these messianic prophecies, and the crowds recognized it immediately. For three years rumors had been swirling around about Jesus' identity. The central question in people's minds was, "Is Jesus the Messiah?" From time to time, he made statements that seemed to confirm this identification, but he was vague enough to keep the authorities guessing. Now there was no mistaking his message. The Messiah had come! They began laying down their outer cloaks and palm branches in the road; it was like they were rolling out a red carpet for their King! The people spontaneously broke out in shouts, quoting the Messianic cry of the very Hallel Psalm they had been singing on the way, *"Hosanna! Blessed is he who comes in the name of the Lord!"* (See Psalm 118:25-26.)

Hosanna is the Hebrew word that means "God save us!" When people saw Jesus make this Messianic statement, they were filled with the hope he would be the one to finally throw off their Roman occupiers and establish a kingdom of justice and peace for them. This was the salvation they were longing for. When they cried out, *"Blessed is the coming kingdom of our father David! Hosanna in the highest heaven!"* they expressed their expectation that the Messiah would establish a new government in Jerusalem.

They were right that Jesus came as the fulfillment of God's promise to David to raise up his Son who would establish an eternal Kingdom. But they didn't understand the nature of their King or his Kingdom. They didn't understand that Jesus was coming, not just as a Jewish king, but as the King of the Universe. They didn't understand that he was coming, not as a military conqueror, but to lay down his life in love as the perfect sacrifice to take away the sin of the world. They didn't understand his Kingdom was not going to be the government over a certain territory, but a movement that would change all human history and ultimately usher in a whole new creation!

What kind of salvation do you need from Jesus? What does it mean for you to honor him as your true King?

Reflect and Respond
What is Jesus saying to me right now?

What step of faith is Jesus calling me to take today?

Footsteps Every Week: Review

Write a brief summary of what Jesus said to you each day this past week and the step of faith he called you to take:

Monday

Tuesday

Wednesday

Thursday

Friday

Saturday

Footsteps Every Week: Reflect

Big Picture
As you look over what Jesus has said to you this past week, do you see any themes? What is the most important thing you need to remember and believe?

Predictable Pattern
As you look over what Jesus called you to do this past week, is there a new predictable pattern he is inviting you to establish in your life with God and others?

Plant the Word
As you look over the readings from this past week, write out the passage that feels most important for you and memorize it over the next week:

DAY 43

READ AND LISTEN: MARK 11:12-25
Take a minute to listen for what the Spirit is saying in these verses…

COMMENT AND CONSIDER
Each morning Jesus and his disciples walked over the Mount of Olives from Bethany to the Temple, where Jesus taught and healed. Each evening they returned to Bethany to spend the night with the extended family of Mary, Martha, and Lazarus. Mark tells us this was their daily rhythm during this final week in Jerusalem. The second morning, as they left Bethany, they passed a fig tree. When Jesus looked for fruit and found none, he cursed the tree. This seems a strange detail for Mark to record, until we realize Jesus was following the pattern of the great prophets of Israel who often carried out symbolic acts as an expression of God's message to the people.

When pilgrims entered the Temple courts, four concentric barriers surrounded the Temple, restricting access. The outer courts were open to anyone, even Gentiles. Closer to the Temple was a fence with signs in Hebrew, Greek, and Latin warning Gentiles not to come any closer at the pain of death. Beyond this was the Court of the Women, where both male and female Jews could enter if they had carried out the appropriate purity rites. Then came the Court of Israel where only Jewish men could go when taking an animal to be sacrificed. The Court of Priests was limited to the priests who offered sacrifices, and then came the Sanctuary of the Temple itself, where only the priest selected for that day was allowed to enter. The Holy of Holies was separated from the Sanctuary by a huge curtain, where only the High Priest could enter once a year on the Day of Atonement.

When Jesus entered the Temple courts, he did something even more strange than cursing the fig tree. He began overturning the tables of those who were exchanging money for people to pay the Temple tax and the chairs of those selling sacrificial doves. While doing this, he quoted the Prophets Isaiah and Jeremiah: *"Is it not written, My house will be called a house of prayer for all nations? But you have made it a den of thieves!"* (See Isaiah 56:7 and Jeremiah 7:11.)

It is often assumed Jesus was driving secular merchants out of a sacred precinct, but these were services worshipers needed when they came to the Temple, and this was the place designated for such activities. Some have wondered if these merchants were overcharging pilgrims and Jesus was trying to reform their practice. But if Jesus were actually trying to change Temple practice, it would have caught the attention of the Roman soldiers stationed in the Antonia Fortress on the northwest corner of the Temple courts. As they did when there was a disturbance over Paul's visit to the Temple (see Acts 21:30-36), they would have come storming onto the Temple plaza to violently put down any disturbance. But Jesus' action did not provoke such a response, which indicates this was a smaller, symbolic action.

Like the biblical prophets of old, Jesus demonstrated God's judgment of the Temple rituals which had become an externalized, legalistic system rather than a genuine engagement with God. He demonstrated against the exclusivism that restricted access to the presence of God. When Solomon dedicated the Temple, he prayed people would come from every nation of the world to meet God in the Temple and worship him there. (See 1 Kings 8:41-43.) Now they were threatening to kill people if they came too close!

The next morning the disciples saw that the fig tree Jesus had cursed was withered to its very roots. This was a picture of what was going to happen to the Temple because it had become a fruitless tree. Forty years later the Romans completely destroyed the Temple, and it has never been rebuilt. Are you stuck in any fruitless religious practices that are not helping you draw nearer to God's presence? Are you putting up barriers that are keeping others from experiencing God's love? What tables and chairs do you need to ask Jesus to turn over in your life today?

Reflect and Respond

What is Jesus saying to me right now?

What step of faith is Jesus calling me to take today?

DAY 44

READ AND LISTEN: MARK 11:27-33
Take a minute to listen for what the Spirit is saying in these verses...

COMMENT AND CONSIDER
Authority is having the power to enact your will. When you say something, it happens. When you do something, it is effective. Authority is one of the defining characteristics of Jesus. When people met him, watched him, and listened to him, they were often amazed by his authority. When Jesus taught from the Scriptures, he did not appeal to the interpretation of other rabbis but spoke directly as a representative of his Father the King. When Jesus spoke to demons, they fled. When Jesus rebuked sickness, people were healed. When Jesus touched those considered unclean, they were made clean.

Other leaders at Jesus' time wielded authority. The Romans had imperial authority on the basis of their Legions. The Herodians had political authority on the basis of their loyalty to Rome. The Sadducees had authority through the sacrificial system at the Temple. The Pharisees had authority because of their knowledge of the Law. The source of the authority determined the kind of power the one authorized can exercise.

Jesus' authority came from his relationship with the Father. Jesus knew he was the beloved Son of his heavenly Father. Jesus knew his heavenly Father was the King of the Universe. Jesus was completely submitted to the will of his Father the King. The reason Jesus could do supernatural things is because he exercised the authority of his Father the King who has all authority in heaven and earth. This is also why Jesus was so threatening to the groups who exercised less powerful authority. The Romans were worried Jesus would lead a rebellion against their rule. The Herodians were worried the Romans would strip them of local power. The Pharisees were worried Jesus' teaching would undermine their own system of religious rules and rituals.

When Jesus overturned the tables of the moneychangers and the chairs of those selling animals in the Temple courts, it was a prophetic demonstration that directly challenged the authority of the religious leaders in Jerusalem. That is why they confronted Jesus the next day in the Temple Courts, asking him by what authority he was doing these things. Jesus knew they were trying to trick him into making a claim they could use as an excuse to arrest him. So rather than fall into their trap, he responded with a question of his own, *"I will ask you one question; then answer me, and I will tell you by what authority I do these things. Was John's baptism from heaven or of human origin? Answer me."*

These religious leaders rightly understood if they admitted John's authority came from God, they would only reinforce Jesus' authority because John pointed people to Jesus. On the other hand, if they denied his authority came from God, it would provoke the Passover crowds, because John was so widely acknowledged as a true prophet of God. And so, Jesus brilliantly beat them at their own game, silencing their manipulative questions while being true to his own identity and authority.

When we read of Jesus' authority it is easy to attribute it to his divinity and therefore exempt ourselves from learning to exercise that kind of authority ourselves. But Jesus showed us that we too are the beloved daughters and sons of the King who also have been given the authority and power to do God's will through the Spirit. When he sent his disciples out on mission he explicitly passed on to them the authority and power he received from the Father. (See Mark 3:14-15.) That is why they were able to do the things Jesus did! When he commissioned them to make disciples the way he did, he passed on to them *"all authority... in heaven and on earth."* (Matthew 28:18)

Where does your authority come from? How can you intentionally step into the authority given to you as a son/daughter of the King today so you can do his will more effectively?

REFLECT AND RESPOND
What is Jesus saying to me right now?

What step of faith is Jesus calling me to take today?

DAY 45

READ AND LISTEN: MARK 12:1-12
Take a minute to listen for what the Spirit is saying in these verses...

COMMENT AND CONSIDER

The primary crops in first-century Palestine were grains, olives, grapes, figs, and dates. In that arid climate, clean water was scarce, and most extended families collected rainwater in underground cisterns. This water often became stagnant, grew algae, and contained parasites. To keep from being sickened by fouled water, the primary drink for everyday life was wine mixed with water because the alcohol killed the germs and parasites. This is one of the reasons vineyards were a common feature of life in Jesus' world.

In this parable Jesus describes the construction of a classic vineyard in Israel, many of which have been discovered from biblical times. The ground was cleared of stones, and rows of vines were planted. The stones were used to build a wall around the vineyard to protect it from animals, and to build a watchtower to keep a lookout for thieves. They built a plastered platform where the grapes could be crushed by bare feet. Next to this winepress they dug a pit where the juice was collected, then transferred into clay jars or wineskins.

It was not unusual for a wealthy landowner to build a vineyard and lease it to tenants who operated the vineyard, kept a portion of the harvest for themselves, and paid a portion back to the owner as rent. Jesus drew on this familiar scenario to tell a scandalous story. When the owner sent his servants to collect his portion of the harvest, they were beaten and sent back empty-handed, while some were killed. The exaggerated patience and forbearance of the owner is highlighted by his decision to keep sending more and more servants who were beaten and/or killed. Finally, the owner decided to solve the problem by sending his beloved son who carried the authority of his father, knowing they would never dare to harm his son. But that is exactly what they did, thinking they could eliminate the future heir and take ownership of the vineyard themselves.

It is such a shocking scenario that the deeper meaning of this prophetic parable was crystal clear to Jesus' hearers. The people of Israel were often depicted as the vineyard of the Lord in the Hebrew Bible. (See Isaiah 5:1-7.) The leaders of Jerusalem had a nasty habit of rejecting and even executing prophets who brought convicting messages they did not like. Jesus repeatedly referred to himself as *"the Son of Man,"* and others recognized him as *"the Son of God."* When the owner sent his son, Jesus clearly referenced himself, particularly after his obviously messianic entry into the city on a donkey a few days earlier.

The crowds on the Mount of Olives quoted Psalm 118:25-26 when Jesus made his triumphal entry, and now Jesus quoted from verses 22-23: *"The stone that the builders rejected has become the cornerstone."* In Aramaic the wordplay would have been obvious because the word for *"stone"* (*eben*) sounded so much like the word for *"son"* (*ben*). Of course, Jesus prophesied the impending rejection, abuse, and death he was about to suffer from the leaders of Jerusalem. Perhaps no one knew it then, but later the disciples realized the stone of Golgotha on which Jesus was crucified is a rocky outcropping left by the rebuilders of the Temple when they quarried around a section of limestone that was unsuitable for building. Jesus was literally crucified on the stone that the builders rejected! It is hard to imagine a more poignant fulfillment of prophecy than that! (See Acts 4:8-12.) And through Jesus' death and resurrection he laid the cornerstone of a whole new reality that is coming—the New Creation, the eternal Kingdom of God.

Do you find it hard to accept those who bring you a challenging message? In what ways are you prone to rejecting the message by rejecting the messenger? What does it mean to recognize Jesus as the cornerstone of your life?

Reflect and Respond

What is Jesus saying to me right now?

What step of faith is Jesus calling me to take today?

DAY 46

READ AND LISTEN: MARK 12:13-17

Take a minute to listen for what the Spirit is saying in these verses…

COMMENT AND CONSIDER

Each day during the week leading up to the Passover, Jesus and his disciples walked over the Mount of Olives from Bethany into Jerusalem where he gathered with large crowds eager to hear his teachings or be healed by him. The huge plaza Herod the Great had built around the Temple was surrounded by a magnificent portico nearly a mile long. The outer wall was solid stone with a porch roof overhead supported by a double row of 30-foot-tall stone columns. This created a large space where people could gather, protected from sun in the summer and rain in the winter. The back wall and roof reflected the sound of a teacher's voice, providing amplification for a large group of people. It is in one of these great porticoes that Jesus taught the crowds and faced the religious leaders who were determined to trap Jesus with their questions.

The Pharisees and Herodians were normally political enemies, but they were united In their fear of Jesus' authority and desire to eliminate him. The Romans imposed heavy taxation on income, property, and trade, as well as the poll tax (or "head tax"), a fixed amount charged for every adult living under Roman occupation. This was the most hated of all Roman taxes because it implied that Rome had taken ownership of the land, and all the people as well. To make it worse, this tax supported the Roman Legions who had conquered and were now oppressing the people of Israel.

The imposition of this poll tax in AD 6 touched off the short-lived rebellion led by Judas the Galilean, who exhorted the Jews of Galilee not to pay it and burned the homes of families who did. Judas' followers became known as the Zealots, a group of religious nationalists determined to overthrow the Romans and anyone aligned with them. The Zealots taught that paying taxes to Rome was treason against the Jewish people.

On the other hand, the Herodians and Sadducees cooperated closely with the Romans and relied on social stability and the collection of taxes to maintain their power. Anyone who openly taught Jews not to pay their taxes was immediately branded a rebel and made liable to the full force of Roman justice. The Herodians and Pharisees attempted to trap Jesus by asking him the loaded question, *"Is it lawful to pay taxes to Caesar or not? Should we pay or shouldn't we?"* If he said yes, he would be labeled a traitor to the Jews, if he said no he would be branded a rebel against Rome.

Jesus, fully aware of their hypocritical scheme, asked them for a denarius, the standard silver coin that was equal to a day's wages. One side depicted Tiberias Caesar with the inscription labeling him the "DIVINE AUGUSTUS." The other side featured his wife Livia seated on a throne and dressed as a pagan priestess. Using this obviously idolatrous prop, Jesus gave his profound answer, *"Give to Caesar the things that are Caesar's, and to God the things that are God's."* Drawing on the language of creation in Genesis, Jesus pointed out that the coin bore the image of Caesar and therefore belonged to Caesar, and thus taxes were to be paid to Rome. On the other hand, as God's children, we bear the very image of the true Creator of the Universe, and we are to give all we are and all we have to him. Jesus shows us how to live in a fallen, pagan world without participating in the idolatry of that world.

Where does your allegiance lie? Do your priorities and actions demonstrate that you have given yourself wholly to represent the God whose image you bear? Or have you slipped into paying unholy allegiance to the idolatry of this fallen world?

Reflect and Respond

What is Jesus saying to me right now?

What step of faith is Jesus calling me to take today?

DAY 47

READ AND LISTEN: MARK 12:18-27

Take a minute to listen for what the Spirit is saying in these verses…

COMMENT AND CONSIDER

Since the Herodians and Pharisees failed to trap Jesus with their trick question, the Sadducees decided to give it a try. The Sadducees were the aristocratic priests of Jerusalem who ran the sacrificial system at the Temple. The Pharisees were committed to teaching and following all the books of the Hebrew Bible, but the Sadducees only recognized the Torah, the first five books of the Law, as authoritative Scripture. That means they did not believe in the resurrection of the dead or a personal existence in the afterlife because those were revealed in the later books of the Bible.

Jesus recognized the truth and authority of the entire Hebrew Bible, and his teaching was closer to the Pharisees who believed in angels and demons, the resurrection, and an eternal afterlife in the renewed creation. However, Jesus did not recognize the authority of the oral traditions of the rabbis, which the Pharisees considered equal to Scripture. With this in mind, the Sadducees tried to trap Jesus in a theological conundrum by asking him a question about the resurrection.

In Deuteronomy 25:5-6 Moses gave instruction that if a man died childless, one of his brothers in the extended family was to marry his brother's widow and have children with her to carry on the deceased brother's lineage. This is called "levirate marriage." With this in mind, the Sadducees described a scenario in which seven brothers died, one at a time, with each one marrying the widow of the one who died before him. In the end this woman would have been married to all seven of them. And so, they asked him *"In the resurrection, when they rise, whose wife will she be, since the seven had married her?"* They were trying to portray the resurrection as incompatible with Moses' teaching.

As usual, Jesus' brilliant response completely transcended the question and avoided the intended trap! First, he pointed out the reason their teaching is flawed is because they didn't actually know the Scriptures. They didn't recognize the authority of the Hebrew Bible and so their teaching was built on a flawed foundation. It was by his Word that God called all things into being out of nothing in creation. (See Genesis 1:1-2:3.) Jesus himself is the Word made flesh. (See John 1:1-5, 14.) As Isaiah 40:8 says, *"The grass withers, the flowers fade, but the word of our God remains forever."* Only by recognizing the Scriptures as the Word of God, reading that Word, studying its meaning, and submitting to its truth, will we have a solid foundation on which to build our lives.

But Jesus said just studying the Word alone is not enough; we also need the power of God's Spirit to understand and respond to God's Word. The Holy Spirit was hovering over the waters of creation when God spoke it all into existence. The Holy Spirit was poured out on Jesus when he launched his public mission by submitting to baptism. The Holy Spirit filled the disciples on the day of Pentecost and sent them to the ends of the earth with the Good News of the Kingdom. Without the Spirit we cannot rightly understand the truth of Scripture. Without yielding to the Spirit, we will never be able to put that truth into action.

Jesus said the wise person who builds their house on the rock is the one who both hears the Word and does it. (See Matthew 7:24-27.) Paul said that faith comes from hearing Jesus' personal word spoken to our hearts. (See Romans 10:17.) Do you recognize and submit to the whole Word of God in the Bible? Are you both learning to know the Word and exercise the faith it creates in you by the power of the Spirit?

Reflect and Respond
What is Jesus saying to me right now?

What step of faith is Jesus calling me to take today?

DAY 48

READ AND LISTEN: MARK 12:28-34

Take a minute to listen for what the Spirit is saying in these verses…

COMMENT AND CONSIDER

Initially this teacher approached Jesus in order to test him. (See Matthew 22:35.) But he was also drawn by the depth and brilliance of Jesus' insights. His question was an honest one rather than a trap. For centuries the rabbis had debated the relative weight of the many different commandments. They divided the biblical commands into light and heavy commandments. One rabbi taught there were 365 negative commands and 248 positive commands.

Jesus answered by quoting one of the most famous passages in the Hebrew Bible, familiar because it was recited every morning and every evening by devout Jews, *"The most important is 'Listen, Israel! The Lord our God, the Lord is one. Love the Lord your God with all your heart, with all your soul, with all your mind, and with all your strength.' This is the greatest and most important command."* By highlighting Deuteronomy 6:4-5, Jesus pointed us to love as the central principle of God and his purpose in creation.

God created human beings in his own image. (See Genesis 1:27.) This is a picture of the closest and most loving human relationship there is, the love between a parent and a child. He gave human beings free will because genuine love has to be freely chosen. If love is coerced, it is not really love, but slavish obedience. Even though his children chose to reject him and go their own way, God refuses to give up on us and keeps calling us back to himself with stubborn, unrelenting love. John tells us the very nature of God is love and there is no way to know him or relate to him except in love. (See 1 John 4:7-19.) Jesus shows us that receiving God's love and reciprocating that love is the most important thing in all of life and all of creation.

But Jesus didn't stop there. He went on to quote a much more obscure passage from Leviticus 19:18, *"The second is, 'Love your neighbor as yourself.' There is no other command greater than these."* The scribe didn't ask for the top two, but for the most important one, yet Jesus gave him two because they are inseparable. You cannot do the first without also doing the second. We are not to love others instead of ourselves, but in the same way that we naturally seek what is best for ourselves we are also to seek the best for others. Sometimes this means sacrificing what we want for the sake of the other, but it does not mean denigrating our own worth and value as children of God.

At the last supper Jesus told the disciples, *"I give you a new command: Love one another. Just as I have loved you, you are also to love one another."* (John 13:34) Jesus made it clear his love for the disciples was to be both the model of and the source of their love for one another. As Jesus demonstrated, this is not just a love for other disciples, but a love freely given to every human being on the planet! It is not the individual commandments to love God and love our neighbor that make this such a brilliant answer, but the connection between loving God and loving others that gives us such powerful insight into what life is really meant to be. Are you receiving the great love God has for you as his beloved child? Are you freely reciprocating that love to God or slipping into a kind of slavish obedience? How does your relationship with the God who is love empower you to love others as you love yourself?

Reflect and Respond

What is Jesus saying to me right now?

What step of faith is Jesus calling me to take today?

Footsteps Every Week: Review

Write a brief summary of what Jesus said to you each day this past week and the step of faith he called you to take:

Monday

Tuesday

Wednesday

Thursday

Friday

Saturday

Footsteps Every Week: Reflect

Big Picture
As you look over what Jesus has said to you this past week, do you see any themes? What is the most important thing you need to remember and believe?

Predictable Pattern
As you look over what Jesus called you to do this past week, is there a new predictable pattern he is inviting you to establish in your life with God and others?

Plant the Word
As you look over the readings from this past week, write out the passage that feels most important for you and memorize it over the next week:

DAY 49

READ AND LISTEN: MARK 12:35-44

Take a minute to listen for what the Spirit is saying in these verses…

COMMENT AND CONSIDER

While Jesus taught in the Temple courts, Mark says *"the large crowd was listening to him with delight."* Something about the way Jesus communicated the Good News of the Kingdom filled people with a sense of joy. This was in sharp contrast to the often harsh and burdensome teaching they received from the scribes and Pharisees. Perhaps part of their delight came from Jesus' refusal to be intimidated by the aggressive posture of these religious leaders and his obviously superior intellectual and spiritual authority.

After fielding the religious and political leaders' loaded questions, Jesus posed a question of his own. He quoted Psalm 110, which was widely read as David speaking of his messianic descendent, *"David himself says by the Holy Spirit: The Lord declared to my Lord, 'Sit at my right hand until I put your enemies under your feet.'"* *The Lord* in this passage is God, and *my Lord* is the coming Messiah. This was taken to mean that the Messiah, a human descendant of David, would be seated at the right hand of God, who would crush Israel's enemies. But Jesus pointed out that it doesn't make sense for the Messiah to be merely human if David, the older ancestor, refers to him as *"my Lord."* Jesus pointed to the divinity of the Messiah and, by extension, hinted at his own divinity.

In addition to challenging the theology of the religious leaders, Jesus also confronted their hypocrisy. Middle Eastern culture was and is an honor/shame culture. This means that people are generally valued by the level of honor they inspire for themselves and their family, minus the amount of shame they heap on themselves and those close to them. Jesus pointed out various external measures of honor in that culture that the Pharisees loved, such as the long white robes by which they set themselves apart from others. Laborers generally wore short robes with short sleeves to allow freedom of movement for manual labor, whereas those of higher socio-economic rank generally wore long robes with long sleeves. The synagogues had rows of built-in seating around the perimeter for the elite, while most people sat on the floor. In a banquet, the closer you sat to the host, the higher the honor paid to you. The Pharisees were known for their extravagant displays of public piety, but Jesus said they would be judged for seeking to build up their own honor while extorting from widows who were on the financial margins.

Mark tied in Jesus' criticism of religious pride to a powerful event involving a vulnerable widow. Jesus sat in the Court of the Women, one of the inner courts of the Temple, which had thirteen bronze chests with trumpet-shaped openings on the top. Rich people dropped large amounts of coins into these offering chests through the funnel-shaped openings, making a loud clattering noise and drawing attention to themselves. But Jesus noticed a poor widow quietly standing by one of the freewill offering chests. She slipped in *"two tiny coins worth very little"* (Greek: *lepta*). These were the least valuable coins in circulation, worth 1/64th of a day's wages, and Jesus said this was her total net worth. Jesus commended this woman's generosity and faith as far greater than the large donors' because *"they all gave out of their surplus, but she out of her poverty has put in everything she had—all she had to live on."*

In what ways are you motivated by wanting others to think well of you? Do you slip into the trap of displaying your religion for the approval of others while overlooking acts of true justice that demonstrate your faith?

Reflect and Respond

What is Jesus saying to me right now?

What step of faith is Jesus calling me to take today?

DAY 50

READ AND LISTEN: MARK 13:1-13
Take a minute to listen for what the Spirit is saying in these verses…

COMMENT AND CONSIDER
When Herod remodeled the Temple and expanded the courts around it, he created a complex so large and beautifully constructed that people who visited Jerusalem were in awe of the sacred architecture. The tallest walls of the Temple Mount soared some 165 feet in the air. The plaza they enclosed is the size of 25 American football fields. The largest stones in the retaining walls are over 40 feet long and weigh over 600 tons! No wonder the disciples from rural Galilee strained to look up and said, *"Teacher, look! What massive stones! What impressive buildings!"* Even today the ancient remains of the Temple platform still evoke wonder in visitors. But Jesus responded to his awestruck disciple, *"Do you see these great buildings? Not one stone will be left upon another—all will be thrown down."*

When Jesus sat down with the disciples on the Mount of Olives looking out over this enormous structure, the disciples naturally thought about the end of the world. The Psalmist recorded God's description of the Temple: *"This is my resting place forever."* (Psalm 132:14) They assumed the destruction of the Temple would mark the end of the world, so Jesus' four closest disciples asked him privately, *"Tell us, when will these things happen? And what will be the sign when all these things are about to be accomplished?"* Jesus responded by warning them not to overreact, even to dramatic events such as wars, earthquakes, and famines. These are just the beginning of a process that will eventually culminate in the end of the world. This is a reminder to be skeptical of preachers who interpret current events as evidence that the end is imminent.

Jesus warned them of such false messengers: *"Watch out that no one deceives you. Many will come in my name, saying, 'I am he,' and they will deceive many.* At Jesus' time messianic pretenders came and went nearly every generation. When he was ten, Judas the Galilean led a revolt that was violently crushed by the Romans. The first-century Jewish historian Josephus claimed messianic expectation was the primary cause of the first great Jewish revolt that resulted in the Roman legions burning Jerusalem and destroying literally every structure on the great Temple Mount. In the early second century, another so-called Messiah, Simon Bar Kochba, led the second great Jewish revolt, resulting in a similar Roman conquest, but this time all the Jews and Jewish followers of Jesus were exiled from Jerusalem.

Jesus warned them that these tumultuous events would include persecution from the Jewish religious leaders as well as Roman governors and emperors. Even family members would turn them over to the authorities for execution. Jesus explained that these extreme events would actually become opportunities for them to declare and demonstrate the Good News of the Kingdom through their response. He promised the Holy Spirit would give them strength and the right words to say at the right time. In the end those who persevere will overcome: *"the one who endures to the end will be saved."*

Jesus prepared his disciples for the challenges that lay ahead. He didn't want them over-reacting to difficult and disorienting events. He didn't want them to be deceived and carried away by unfounded teaching and untrustworthy leaders. He wanted to help them prepare for trying times so they could endure and be effective witnesses to the Good News of God's coming Kingdom. Are you prepared for the challenges that lie ahead? Are you willing to endure the inevitable trials that will come? Are you ready to be an effective witness even in the face of opposition and hostility?

REFLECT AND RESPOND

What is Jesus saying to me right now?

What step of faith is Jesus calling me to take today?

DAY 51

READ AND LISTEN: MARK 13:14-27
Take a minute to listen for what the Spirit is saying in these verses…

COMMENT AND CONSIDER
There are often two horizons in biblical prophecy. The near horizon prepares us for challenging events that will soon take place. The far horizon gives us perspective on the big picture, whether or not we ever experience the things that will one day take place. Jesus' apocalyptic teaching on the Mount of Olives had a near horizon, meant to prepare the first and second generations of his followers in Jerusalem for the momentous challenges that were soon to come. It also had a far horizon, meant to help us understand where history is headed and the climactic events which will one day take place, although the timing and details remain a mystery.

As the religious and political leaders carried out persecutions against the followers of Jesus in the decades following his resurrection and ascension, these men and women must have drawn strength from Jesus' prophetic warnings and promises. As the Zealot movement grew in popularity and tensions grew with Rome, they must have been carefully reflecting on Jesus' words about false prophets, wars, and rumors of wars. When the Tenth Legion conquered Jerusalem in AD 70, Roman soldiers set up pagan symbols on the Temple Mount, and General Titus entered the Holy of Holies, the followers of Jesus must have remembered his words, *"When you see the abomination of desolation standing where it should not be then those in Judea must flee to the mountains."* According to the historian Eusebius, the followers of Jesus did flee to Pella and were saved the fate of so many who were killed in the city.

But these words were also spoken and written for our benefit. Many centuries have come and gone since the destruction of Jerusalem and we still are reminded not to overreact to tumultuous events, not to be deceived by false prophets, and not to be surprised when governments or even family members actively oppose the sharing of Jesus' Good News. This is our near horizon.

But the time is coming when the far horizon will draw near, the final *"abomination of desolation"* will take place, and then the signs of Jesus' return will become obvious. Cosmic events far greater than earthquakes or wars will signal the end has finally come. The sun's fire will burn out, the moon will have no light to reflect, and the stars will begin to fall like tears from heaven. When these cosmic signs reveal the time has finally come, Jesus himself, the heavenly Son of Man described in Daniel 7, will appear on clouds in glory and usher in the completed Kingdom of God in a cosmic conflagration and re-creation of all things!

Inasmuch as the near horizon prepares us for what we will soon have to endure, the far horizon gives us hope for the future. We know how the story ends! We don't know when and we don't know exactly how, but we know Jesus is the victorious King of kings who will reign forever and ever. We don't have to live in fear because we know our Redeemer lives, and at the end *"he will stand on the dust,"* and we will see God with our own eyes! (See Job 19:25-27.) And in that day, whether we are still alive on earth or have fallen asleep in death, the angels will gather all of us who know Jesus and are part of God's family, and we will be together forever in God's renewed creation where Jesus will reign forever in perfect love, justice, and peace!

How does the near horizon of Jesus' apocalyptic teaching help you prepare for the inevitable challenges? How does the far horizon of Jesus' completed victory give you hope in the present and peace for the future?

Reflect and Respond

What is Jesus saying to me right now?

What step of faith is Jesus calling me to take today?

DAY 52

READ AND LISTEN: MARK 13:28-37

Take a minute to listen for what the Spirit is saying in these verses…

COMMENT AND CONSIDER

Most trees in Palestine do not lose their leaves in the winter, except for the fig tree. The appearance of buds on the bare branches of a fig tree is an unmistakable sign of spring, and soon the unfurling of broad fig leaves signals the arrival of summer. On both the near horizon and the far horizon of biblical prophecy, we will watch signs indicating when these events are ready to take place, and we can learn to read the signs, just like we can watch for a fig tree's buds. But there is a difference between recognizing the signs and predicting the timing. The early followers of Jesus assumed all the things Jesus prophesied on the Mount of Olives that day would take place within their lifetime.

It was true of the near horizon events. Most of them faced severe persecution. The Holy Spirit did give them the words to say when they were dragged before religious and political rulers. The fall of Jerusalem did happen within the lifetime of that generation. But these early followers of Jesus assumed there was only a near horizon and Jesus would return soon, or at least within their lifetime. Of course, they were wrong. Jesus was crystal clear that no one knows the day or the hour when the far horizon will finally come, not the angels, not even Jesus. Only the Father in heaven knows!

Jesus told a simple parable about the unpredictability of his return. It is like a man who gave clear responsibilities to the slaves in his household and went away, not telling them when he would return. His mandate was for each of them to faithfully fulfill their role and keep watch for his unexpected return. This faithful watchfulness is the posture we are to take as Jesus' followers. It doesn't mean we simply sit on the rooftop staring at the horizon waiting for our master's return. That would be irresponsible. Instead, we carry out our assignments with the realization that our master might walk in the door at any moment!

It is so easy to fall asleep on our watch, like the disciples did in the Garden of Gethsemane. Their mandate was to watch and pray, but they drifted off and forgot their task. Jesus said, *"Stay awake and pray so that you won't enter into temptation. The spirit is willing, but the flesh is weak."* (Mark 14:38) This world has a powerful pull that lulls us into sleepiness. We lose our focus, forget our assignment, and end up asleep at the wheel. Paul exhorted the followers of Jesus in Ephesians, who would eventually lose their first love, by quoting the ancient exhortation, *"Get up, sleeper, and rise up from the dead, and Christ will shine on you."* (Ephesians 5:14)

What is lulling you to sleep right now? How can Jesus' promise to return rouse you from slumber? What does it mean for you to be faithfully watchful and ready for Jesus' return?

Reflect and Respond

What is Jesus saying to me right now?

What step of faith is Jesus calling me to take today?

DAY 53

READ AND LISTEN: MARK 14:1-11

Take a minute to listen for what the Spirit is saying in these verses…

COMMENT AND CONSIDER

The Passover meal with roasted lamb, was held on the 15th of Nisan in the Jewish calendar. The following day began a weeklong holiday called the Festival of the Unleavened Bread. This second holiday was an opportunity for those who could not travel to Jerusalem or afford a lamb for sacrifice to celebrate Passover without the sacrificial animal. In Jerusalem the two were typically celebrated as one eight-day holiday. As Passover drew near, the religious leaders decided to wait and arrest Jesus after the actual eve of Passover was over, so the crowds would be distracted and less likely to cause a riot when Jesus was put to death.

With this ominous backdrop, Mark tells us of a special banquet put on in Bethany by a friend of Jesus called Simon the Leper. A banquet was served on a low, three-sided table (Latin: *triclinium*) surrounded with pillows or low couches where the guests reclined on their left elbow with their feet extended away from the table. Normally it was impossible for a leper to host a party because they were strictly required to separate themselves from their own family and any other social contact. This means Simon must have been healed by Jesus at some point and this banquet was his way of thanking Jesus for such an inexpressible gift. John tells us that Lazarus, recently raised from the dead, was also a guest at this banquet, while his sister Martha was helping the other women to cook and serve the meal. (See John 12:1-7.)

Martha's sister Mary made the socially risky decision to join the banquet. Normally only men attended a banquet with guests from outside the extended family, while the women and slaves would serve the meal. The exception would be women providing entertainment or prostitutes. But Mary had a specific purpose in mind and decided to flout social custom by entering the banquet carrying *"an alabaster jar of very expensive perfume of pure nard."* Nard was an extremely expensive plant imported from India used to scent perfumed oils. Such perfume was often kept in small, long-necked bottles made of translucent calcite stone. The fact that Mary broke the neck of the bottle means she was planning to pour out all of it, worth a whole year's salary!

In the hot, dry Middle East, it is considered a blessing to rub soothing and protective oil on your face and hair. Conscientious hosts often provided special oil for guests to anoint themselves upon arriving for the meal. We experience this still today at restaurants in traditional Middle Eastern settings when we are offered lemon-scented oil to rub on our hands and face after a meal. When Mary poured out this oil on Jesus' head, she followed accepted social customs of honor and blessing, but the amount and value of the perfumed oil was extravagant. It was such a lavish act that some began to criticize her, but Jesus affirmed her for what she did, describing it as a prophetic demonstration of what was soon to happen.

When the wind blew from the east, the smoke of the burnt offerings mixed with the smell of the Temple incense and filled the city of Jerusalem with its distinctive odor of sacrifice and worship. The powerful scent that filled the room that night in Bethany was a similar sign of Jesus' coming sacrifice on the cross and the anointing that would prepare him for burial. Mary offered her most valuable gift as an outward sign of her inexpressible love and devotion to Jesus. Are you willing to flout convention and open yourself up to criticism to openly demonstrate your love for Jesus? What are you willing to give up as an expression of your devotion to him?

Reflect and Respond

What is Jesus saying to me right now?

What step of faith is Jesus calling me to take today?

DAY 54

READ AND LISTEN: MARK 14:12-31
Take a minute to listen for what the Spirit is saying in these verses...

COMMENT AND CONSIDER
When the people of Israel were slaves in Egypt, God sent Moses to set them free. After confronting Pharoah and the people of Egypt with nine dramatic plagues, God warned Moses about the final and most terrible plague, death of the firstborn. He gave the people of Israel a way to make the angel of death "pass over" their homes by spreading the blood of a lamb on the doorposts and lintels of their homes, and then roasting the lamb and eating it with unleavened bread. When the firstborn males of Egypt were struck down, Pharaoh finally relented and released the enslaved Israelites. Thus began their long journey into the Promised Land of Canaan and the tradition of Passover was born. For more than three millennia, the Jewish people have gathered annually to celebrate this covenantal meal and recount the events by which God redeemed the people of Israel.

In the time of Jesus, those who could afford it traveled to Jerusalem for the Passover celebration. On the afternoon of the 14th of Nisan, a male of each extended family took an unblemished lamb up to the Temple and offered it to the priests to be sacrificed. After the blood was sprinkled on the altar, the carcass of the lamb was returned, and they brought it home to be roasted for the Passover meal. The room for the meal was swept of all leaven and they set a low, three-sided table (Latin: *triclinium*). The roasted lamb was served with unleavened bread, bitter herbs, and four cups of wine, while the head of the family recounted the events of the Exodus.

To ensure he was able to celebrate this final Passover meal with the disciples before his arrest, Jesus arranged for Mary, the mother of John Mark, to provide an upper room in their fancy home in the southwest part of Jerusalem where the group could share the meal. He kept the location secret, even from his own disciples, establishing a special sign and password to lead Peter and John to the house where they prepared for the meal.

That night, after they had eaten the roast lamb, Jesus began to reinterpret the meal. He lifted the unleavened bread and said, *"Take it; this is my body."* Then he lifted the third cup, traditionally called the cup of redemption, and said, *"This is my blood of the covenant, which is poured out for many."* Jesus ratified the New Covenant he inaugurated in his baptism. No longer was the broken body and shed blood of a lamb the basis of their redemption. From now on it would be Jesus' body and blood, broken and shed on the cross once and for all, that would be the basis for the redemption of all humanity. Every time we share in this special meal, we claim what Jesus has done for us on the cross and reaffirm our participation in this New Covenant family.

Jesus knew Judas would betray him, Peter would deny him, and they would all desert him. He included them in the meal anyway. The New Covenant of Jesus is not for those who get it all right; it is for us who betray, deny, and desert him in various ways. Through his body and blood we are forgiven and learn to live a new life in him, just as those very fallible first disciples did. How have you failed Jesus? Are you willing to draw near to him anyway? Will you receive his body and blood that alone can strengthen you to live a more Jesus-shaped life?

Reflect and Respond

What is Jesus saying to me right now?

What step of faith is Jesus calling me to take today?

FOOTSTEPS EVERY WEEK: REVIEW

Write a brief summary of what Jesus said to you each day this past week and the step of faith he called you to take:

MONDAY

TUESDAY

WEDNESDAY

THURSDAY

FRIDAY

SATURDAY

Footsteps Every Week: Reflect

Big Picture

As you look over what Jesus has said to you this past week, do you see any themes? What is the most important thing you need to remember and believe?

Predictable Pattern

As you look over what Jesus called you to do this past week, is there a new predictable pattern he is inviting you to establish in your life with God and others?

Plant the Word

As you look over the readings from this past week, write out the passage that feels most important for you and memorize it over the next week:

DAY 55

READ AND LISTEN: MARK 14:32-42

Take a minute to listen for what the Spirit is saying in these verses...

COMMENT AND CONSIDER

After finishing the Passover meal, Jesus and the disciples made their way to the Garden of Gethsemane at the base of the Mount of Olives. Jesus knew he needed supernatural strength to face the final leg of his journey on earth, so he asked three of his closest disciples to come and pray with him among the olive trees. You can still visit the Garden of Gethsemane today. It sits on the lower western slope of the Mount of Olives, just across the Kidron Valley from the Temple Mount and Jerusalem. Although they do not date back to the time of Jesus, the olive trees tended by the Franciscan monks there are over 1,000 years old, the oldest in the world! In that grove stands a large rock traditionally identified as the place where Jesus poured out his heart to the Father that night. Today the rock is the base of the altar in the Church of All Nations, designed to replicate the feeling of being in an olive grove at night.

In Gethsemane we see the humanity of Jesus on full display. His deep-seated survival instinct was screaming at him to do whatever he could to escape the torture and death he knew would soon engulf him. It would have been easy for Jesus to slip over the Mount of Olives in the dark of night and disappear into one of the countless desert valleys that stretch down to the Jordan River in the east. After all, this is where he spent 40 days and nights in the wilderness, and Jesus knew exactly where he could hide and never be found. But Jesus did what he always did; he turned to his heavenly Father in prayer.

Sometimes we think of prayer as sanctified communication with God, so we assume it must be conducted in a respectful and reverential tone with all the right theological nuances. By contrast Jesus' prayer life was refreshingly real and honest. His models were the Psalmists who simply poured their hearts out to God without filtering the good, the bad, or the ugly. Jesus cried out to the Father, expressing his fear and dread, begging the Father to take away the cup before him. There is something profoundly liberating about voicing our deepest feelings, regardless of how they fit or don't fit into our understanding of God's will.

But that is not where Jesus' prayer ended. Having honestly poured out his desire to avoid what he knew was his destiny, Jesus found the courage to surrender his will the Father's: *"Nevertheless, not what I will, but what you will."* Often, we assume prayer is about trying to get God to do what we want him to do. In fact, it is exactly the opposite! Prayer is meant to put us into the place where the Spirit can shape us according to the will of God. Of course, we are to ask God for what we want and feel we need. Jesus taught us to pray, *"Give us today our daily bread."* (Matthew 6:11) But this is just the starting point for us to gain clarity on the will of God.

When we see that what we are praying for is in line with God's will, we find greater faith and courage to keep fighting for his will to be done on earth as it is in heaven. But sometimes as we pray for what we want, we start to see God has something different and better in mind. This is where we find the faith and courage to let go of what we want and embrace the better way of Jesus. Is your prayer life as honest as Jesus' was? Are you praying in a way that will help you gain clarity and surrender more fully to God's will in your life?

REFLECT AND RESPOND

What is Jesus saying to me right now?

What step of faith is Jesus calling me to take today?

DAY 56

READ AND LISTEN: MARK 14:43-52

Take a minute to listen for what the Spirit is saying in these verses…

COMMENT AND CONSIDER

One of the historical questions about the night of Jesus' arrest is exactly where the Last Supper took place. Archaeologists have discovered the foundations of a large, first-century Jewish home on the southwest hill of Jerusalem, at the site traditionally identified as the Upper Room. They also discovered the remains of a series of churches built over that house. Today a 13th-century building stands there with an upstairs room recreating the setting of the original Last Supper. The historical and archaeological evidence points to this site as the location of the house where Jesus made special arrangements to share his last supper with his disciples.

It is amazing that we can have a high degree of certainty about the location of the Last Supper, but Mark gives a unique detail that seems to identify whose house it was. He tells us *"a certain young man, wearing nothing but a linen cloth,"* was in the Garden of Gethsemane when Jesus was arrested. When the soldiers tried to grab him, they were only able to nab the linen sheet, so the young man ran away naked. What a strange detail for Mark to record! None of the other Gospels makes mention of this young man. Who is he and why does Mark include him?

At the time of Jesus' arrest, Mark was a young man living in his extended family's home in Jerusalem. They were a priestly family from Cyprus with a successful merchant business and had built a fancy home in the southwest quarter of Jerusalem, a wealthy priestly neighborhood. Mark's mother Mary was a relative of Joseph Barnabas, one of the leaders of the early church in Jerusalem who teamed up with the Apostle Paul on his first missionary journey. They took with them Barnabas' young nephew, John Mark. (See Acts 13:1-5.)

Judas left the upper room to betray Jesus by telling the religious leaders where they could arrest him, presumably at the site of the upper room.

However, before Judas and the soldiers got there, Jesus and the other disciples departed for the Mount of Olives. When the soldiers arrived at the house in the middle of the night, beating on the outer door and demanding to be let in, they would have woken up the whole family.

If that house was the home of Mary and John Mark's extended family, the young Mark would have been awakened. In the warmer months it was common for people to sleep naked with a linen sheet for bedding. If Mark realized these soldiers were planning to arrest Jesus and he was aware of the normal place on the Mount of Olives where the disciples sometimes spent the night, it makes perfect sense he could have wrapped that linen sheet around his body and tried to get to the Garden of Gethsemane to warn Jesus. However, he didn't get there in time and had to watch as Jesus was betrayed by Judas and arrested by the soldiers. When the soldiers saw him hiding in the bushes and tried to grab him, he ran away naked. It seems Mark wrote himself into the story with this dramatic cameo, which means the Last Supper took place at the family home of Mary and her son John Mark.

Some years later, when Peter was arrested by Herod Agrippa and then miraculously released from prison by angels, Luke tells us he immediately made his way to the home of Mary the mother of John Mark, where the believers were gathered to pray for him. (See Acts 11:6-12.) This account, together with Mark's cameo, seems to confirm that the location of the Last Supper was the home of Mary and John Mark, and that it became the primary place of gathering for the followers of Jesus in Jerusalem.

What do you think you would have done if you were there when Jesus was arrested? How do you handle it when you lack the courage to represent Jesus?

Reflect and Respond

What is Jesus saying to me right now?

What step of faith is Jesus calling me to take today?

DAY 57

Read and Listen: Mark 14:53-65

Take a minute to listen for what the Spirit is saying in these verses…

Comment and Consider

The Sanhedrin was the Jewish council responsible for overseeing religious and civic matters for the Jews of Jerusalem. It was comprised of seventy members drawn from the powerful priestly families of Jerusalem (*"the chief priests"*), the teachers of the Law (*"the scribes"*), and other aristocratic families (*"the elders"*). The High Priest presided over the Sanhedrin as its 71st member. In Jesus' time the High Priests were appointed by the Roman governor who could also depose and replace them at any time. The Roman governor before Pontius Pilate, Valerius Gratus, appointed and deposed four High Priests during his 11-year tenure. Joseph Caiaphas was the High Priest during Jesus' ministry and Pontius Pilate's rule. Caiaphas held the office for 18 years, an indicator of his willingness to do the will of Rome in order to hold on to power. Caiaphas' father-in-law, Annas, was a former High Priest and had five sons who eventually served in that office. He operated for decades as a kind of godfather figure, exercising unofficial power behind the scenes. (See Luke 3:2; John 18:13, 19-24.)

Throughout Jesus' ministry members of the Sanhedrin were threatened by Jesus' popularity and authority, but when Jesus raised Lazarus from the dead, they resolved to put Jesus to death. (See John 11:47-53.) Once Jesus made his messianic statement by riding over the Mount of Olives into Jerusalem on a donkey and then carried out his prophetic act in the Temple Courts, they began to actively plot his death. None of their efforts to create a pretense for arresting Jesus by asking him trick questions in the Temple courts worked, so they decided to arrest him by stealth in the middle of the night.

Once they had arrested Jesus, they wanted to pass judgment on him as quickly as possible, before news of the arrest leaked out to his followers. So they held an improvised proceeding in the extended family home of Annas and Caiaphas. This so-called "trial" was blatantly biased and nothing more than a thinly veiled attempt to frame Jesus for a capital crime he did not commit in order to justify his execution.

According to the rabbinical traditions which were written down about 170 years after the time of Jesus (the Mishnah), six rules governed a capital trial in the Sanhedrin but were not followed in Jesus' trial. These broken rules included no trials at night, no trials on the eve of a festival, starting the trial with reasons for acquittal, at least two witnesses whose testimony agrees, no verdicts passed on the same day as the examination, and meeting in one of the rooms on the Temple Mount ("the Chamber of Hewn Stone") and not in a private home. We don't know if all these rules were in force at the time of Jesus, but certainly some of them were.

Despite their best efforts to find two people who could corroborate any valid evidence against Jesus, they could not. Through all the false accusations, Jesus chose not to defend himself, realizing the guilty verdict was a foregone conclusion. Finally, Caiaphas asked him directly, *"Are you the Messiah, the Son of the Blessed One?"* Jesus could not deny himself, so he answered, *"I am, and you will see the Son of Man seated at the right hand of Power and coming with the clouds of heaven."* This clear reference to his own divinity was enough for the members of the Sanhedrin present to condemn Jesus to death for blasphemy, defined as speaking against the sacred name of God. (See Leviticus 24:16.) However, the Sanhedrin did not have the authority to carry out capital sentences, so they would have to convince Pilate to carry out their contrived execution for them.

Have you ever been falsely accused of something? How did it make you feel? How did you react? What can you learn from Jesus' example?

Reflect and Respond

What is Jesus saying to me right now?

What step of faith is Jesus calling me to take today?

DAY 58

READ AND LISTEN: MARK 14:66-72

Take a minute to listen for what the Spirit is saying in these verses…

COMMENT AND CONSIDER

When Jesus was arrested in Gethsemane, all his followers scattered just as he prophesied. However, Peter and John regrouped, summoned their courage, and followed the soldiers at a distance as they led Jesus back through the Kidron Valley and up the southwest hill to the house of Caiaphas. John's family had some connections to the family of High Priest, so John was able to get Peter and himself into the very courtyard of Caiaphas' house. (See John 18:15-16.) While the sham trial was taking place in one of the upper rooms of this fancy house, Peter was below in the courtyard standing around a charcoal fire with slaves and members of the household staff.

Archaeologists have not yet identified the actual house of Caiaphas, but we do know the area where the chief priests of the Temple had their homes. Surely Caiaphas' house was somewhere in that area on the southwest hill in the same neighborhood as Mary the mother of John Mark. Archaeologists have discovered a huge courtyard house in that neighborhood, referred to as the "palatial mansion," where an extended family of wealthy and powerful priests lived. It had many rooms built around a large central courtyard with private ritual baths, elegant decorations and furnishings, and sweeping views of the Temple Mount. A large upstairs room looked down into the central courtyard, which perfectly matches the account of Jesus' trial and Peter's denials at the house of Caiaphas. We don't have any direct evidence that this is the house of the High Priest, but it is the largest priestly mansion yet discovered from that time, so if it is not the actual house of Caiaphas, his house would have been very similar.

In close proximity and the flickering light of the fire, some began to recognize Peter as a follower of Jesus, which he immediately denied. When he pulled away from the fire, another slave identified him as a disciple of Jesus, but he insisted he was not. Finally, his Aramaic accent gave him away. Galileans were ridiculed as country hicks by the Jerusalem elite. One rabbinical passage depicts a Galilean in Jerusalem asking to buy some clothing (*'amar*). The merchants ridiculed his accent saying, "Foolish Galilean do you mean an 'ass' for riding (*hamā r*), 'wine' to drink (*hamar*), 'wool' for clothing (*'amar*) or a 'lamb' for killing (*immar*)?" When they identified Peter as a follower of Jesus because he was Galilean, he began to curse and swear that he was not. At that moment the cock crowed. Peter suddenly remembered Jesus' prediction of his triple denial and broke down weeping for shame.

It is easy to look down on Peter for his lack of courage and faithfulness to Jesus, but we must not overlook the incredible courage and devotion it took to enter right into the very house where the authorities were accusing Jesus. They could easily have arrested Peter and John in that courtyard and put them on trial alongside Jesus. But despite his best intentions, Peter's courage faltered when he was called upon to represent Jesus and stand with him in his hour of trial. Too often we do the same when called on to give testimony of what Jesus has done in our lives and to identify ourselves as his followers in unsympathetic company.

In the end it boils down to whose approval is more important to us: the approval of God or the approval of people. When have you shown courage to stand with Jesus in challenging contexts? When has your courage faltered? How can you grow as a courageous witness who is unafraid to testify on behalf of Jesus?

Reflect and Respond

What is Jesus saying to me right now?

What step of faith is Jesus calling me to take today?

DAY 59

READ AND LISTEN: MARK 15:1-15
Take a minute to listen for what the Spirit is saying in these verses…

COMMENT AND CONSIDER

Because it was illegal for the Sanhedrin to carry out a capital trial at night, they convened a more official gathering of the Council at first light to rubber stamp the false conviction they handed out in darkness. Repeating their bogus death sentence, they bound Jesus and led him to the Roman governor's residence. Pontius Pilate became Prefect of Judea in AD 26 and ruled for ten years. His headquarters were located at the Palace of Herod out on the Mediterranean coast at Caesarea Maritima, but for the festival of the Passover Pilate came to Jerusalem and took up residence in the huge palace complex dominating the western edge of the city Herod the Great had built for himself some sixty years earlier.

The palace complex was the size of more than six American football fields and was comprised of two huge residential buildings set at either end of an enormous plaza, referred to as *"the Stone Pavement"* (in Aramaic, *Gabbatha*). (John 19:13) The whole complex was built like a fortress with heavy defensive walls, and the north end was guarded by three enormous towers standing up to 145 feet tall. When you enter the Old City of Jerusalem from the west through Jaffa Gate today, the structure on the south side of the complex is a Crusader castle built on the ruins of the north end of Herod's Palace. Still visible is the massive base of the largest of the three defensive towers. The Jewish religious leaders brought Jesus to this fortified palace for another sham trial.

A Roman governor was the chief judge of his province and the sole arbiter of capital cases. They normally made themselves available for public business in the early hours of the morning. In theory, any Roman subject could bring complaints before their governor, who had absolute power to rule in legal matters. Pilate made some very unwise decisions when he first arrived in Judea. First, he placed pagan Roman symbols in the Temple courts, which caused a huge riot until he eventually had to remove them. Then he confiscated funds from the Temple treasury to build an aqueduct from Bethlehem to Jerusalem, which also sparked riots in which many people were killed. Luke reports that during Jesus' ministry *"some people came and reported to [Jesus] about the Galileans whose blood Pilate had mixed with their sacrifices."* (Luke 13:1)

Since keeping the peace was a provincial governor's main job, Pilate had to learn how to navigate the political sensitivities of his Jewish subjects more carefully if he hoped to maintain his position. He built a working partnership with Caiaphas, whom he retained as High Priest his entire tenure, which underscores his desire to cooperate with Caiaphas. Furthermore, Pilate's primary patron in Rome who was responsible for his original appointment, Lucius Sejanus, had fallen under suspicion of treason and was executed in AD 31. This put Pilate in a very precarious political position and intensified the pressure on him to keep the peace, as any bad news making it back to Rome could spell the end of his rule.

Once again Jesus responded to the question of his identity but refused to defend himself against the baseless accusations of the religious leaders. Pilate saw through the manipulations of Caiaphas and tried to find a way to release Jesus without causing a reaction from the people, but the religious leaders stirred up the biased crowd to demand Jesus' death. Pilate knew Jesus was not guilty of a capital crime, but in the end, he caved to the political pressure and knowingly sentenced an innocent man to a torturous death.

When was the last time you knowingly did something wrong because you were afraid of the consequences of doing the right thing? How can Pilate's story help you to choose a different path next time?

Reflect and Respond

What is Jesus saying to me right now?

What step of faith is Jesus calling me to take today?

DAY 60

READ AND LISTEN: MARK 15:16-32
Take a minute to listen for what the Spirit is saying in these verses…

COMMENT AND CONSIDER
Those sentenced to crucifixion were first scourged using a whip with multiple leather strips imbedded with sharp pieces of metal and bone. Scourging often tore the flesh from the victim's back and even exposed the ribcage and internal organs. The purpose of crucifixion was to terrify the population into subjection and prevent revolt. For this reason, victims of crucifixion were led through the streets carrying the horizontal beam of their cross to the place of crucifixion, which was always outside the city in a highly visible place. The first-century rhetorician Quintilian described crucifixion as a Roman deterrent and explained they chose "the most crowded roads where the most people can see and be moved by this fear."

In Jerusalem this was an abandoned rock quarry just outside the western city wall, near the Gennath ("Garden") Gate, which opened to the road leading to Jaffa on the coast. This was where builders cut limestone blocks to rebuild the Temple after the Jews returned from exile in Babylon. A section of limestone was soft and unsuitable for building, so the builders cut around that section, leaving a 20-foot-high rocky outcropping that resembled a human skull. This is *"Golgotha" (which means "Place of the Skull")* where the Roman soldiers were leading Jesus and the crowd on this grisly procession.

Jesus was so weakened by the all-night interrogations and scourging that he collapsed under the weight of the crossbeam, so the soldiers grabbed one of the bystanders, Simon from Cyrene, to carry it for Jesus. Since his name and that of his sons are recorded, it implies they became followers of Jesus and part of the community to whom Mark was writing.

Once they arrived at the rock of Golgotha, Jesus was stretched out on the crossbeam, iron spikes were driven through his wrists, the crossbeam was lifted up and hung on a permanent post, and iron spikes were driven through his heel bones into the post. As a person hung on the cross, the weight of their body pulling down on their arms constricted the muscles around their ribcage, preventing the lungs from expelling the fluids which naturally accumulate. The result was the person's breathing became shallower and shallower. They had to pull up with their arms and push up with their legs to take the pressure off their lungs to get a breath. Doing so caused great pain at the nail wounds and scraped their torn back against the rough wood of the cross as they moved up and down. The cross was a diabolical device by which the victim had to repeatedly torture themselves to breathe as they slowly suffocated.

As Jesus hung naked and in agony between two convicted rebels, the crowd passing by on the road to Jaffa and the religious leaders who had gathered continued to mock Jesus, just as he had prophesied back in Nazareth when he said, *"No doubt you will quote this proverb to me: 'Doctor, heal yourself.'"* (Luke 4:23) All the while the sign above his head which stated his crime declared the truth about Jesus, *"The King of the Jews."* For centuries Rome used the military prowess of its legions and the terror of torture and death to impose its rule, but here God's Anointed King demonstrated the far greater power of self-giving love. The Emperors of Rome are long since dead and powerless, but the transformational love of God which Jesus poured out from the cross has the power to continuing changing billions of lives 2,000 years later.

How is Jesus calling you to take up your cross today? What does it mean to demonstrate God's love to those who don't love you back? What are you willing to sacrifice to be a vessel of Jesus' transforming love?

REFLECT AND RESPOND
What is Jesus saying to me right now?

What step of faith is Jesus calling me to take today?

Footsteps Every Week: Review

Write a brief summary of what Jesus said to you each day this past week and the step of faith he called you to take:

Monday

Tuesday

Wednesday

Thursday

Friday

Saturday

Footsteps Every Week: Reflect

Big Picture

As you look over what Jesus has said to you this past week, do you see any themes? What is the most important thing you need to remember and believe?

Predictable Pattern

As you look over what Jesus called you to do this past week, is there a new predictable pattern he is inviting you to establish in your life with God and others?

Plant the Word

As you look over the readings from this past week, write out the passage that feels most important for you and memorize it over the next week:

DAY 61

READ AND LISTEN: MARK 15:33-40
Take a minute to listen for what the Spirit is saying in these verses…

COMMENT AND CONSIDER

Jesus was brought before Pilate about 6:00 AM, nailed to the cross about 9:00 AM, and around noon the sky turned dark until 3:00 PM. As modern people we are familiar with a solar eclipse, when the moon blocks the light of sun, but for ancient people such events were filled with symbolic meaning. The Prophet Jeremiah described the sun being darkened as an expression of the whole earth going into mourning. (See Jeremiah 4:27-28.) In the darkness Jesus himself cried out from the cross, *"Eloi, Eloi, lemá sabachtháni?" which is translated, "My God, my God, why have you abandoned me?"* Some have associated this "cry of dereliction" theologically, claiming this is the moment when Jesus took on the sin of the world and the Father turned his back on him. However, it seems more accurate to see Jesus continuing his pattern of open and honest prayer to gain faith and courage amidst trial.

Jesus quoted the opening line of Psalm 22 in this cry from the cross. Before there were chapters and numbers attached to Bible passages, people normally referred to an entire psalm by its opening line. Psalm 22 is a psalm of lament in which David cried out to the Lord in a time of great distress. Many of the lines of this psalm seem to prophetically describe what Jesus was experiencing. It is a powerful reminder that Jesus, in his full humanity, was not shielded from any of the pain or horror of the torture he endured for these six long hours.

It is also important to note that the final ten verses of Psalm 22 are a joyful celebration of God's faithfulness and deliverance, culminating in the promise, *"the next generation will be told about the Lord. They will come and declare his righteousness; to a people yet to be born they will declare what he has done."* (Psalm 22:30-31) Jesus was honest about the horror of his suffering and torture which felt like abandonment, but he also looked to his faithful Father for the strength he needed to endure this final leg of his journey. Even in the darkest moments of his suffering, Jesus pointed to the hope and certainty of God's triumph over sin, hell, death, and the devil!

When Jesus spoke the Aramaic word *"Eloi"* ("My God"), it sounded to some like he was calling for Elijah to come. Since Elijah did not die but ascended to heaven, some believed he would come back from heaven and help in times of distress. The offer of sour wine by the soldier was not an act of compassion, but an attempt to keep Jesus conscious and prolong his suffering.

Finally, after six hours of torture, Jesus committed himself to the Father and breathed his last. The massive curtain in the Temple that separated the Holy of Holies from the Sanctuary was torn from top to bottom. This is a powerful demonstration that the sin which separates us from our Holy God is atoned for and now we can *"approach the throne of grace with boldness, so that we may receive mercy and find grace to help us in time of need.* (Hebrews 4:16)

John the Baptist prophesied when he saw Jesus at the Jordan River, *"Look, the Lamb of God, who takes away the sin of the world!"* (John 1:29) Jesus fulfilled his mission by laying down his life as the perfect sacrifice to pay the price we could not afford. On the cross Jesus took away the guilt and shame of our sin, reuniting us with our heavenly Father and his great family forever! What does Jesus' death on the cross mean to you? What is the sin and shame you need to lay at the foot of the cross so you can draw nearer to God?

REFLECT AND RESPOND
What is Jesus saying to me right now?

What step of faith is Jesus calling me to take today?

DAY 62

READ AND LISTEN: MARK 15:40-47
Take a minute to listen for what the Spirit is saying in these verses…

COMMENT AND CONSIDER
One of Jesus' many counter-cultural traits was his affirmation of women and recognition of women as disciples in a society where women were considered second-class citizens at best and the property of men at worst. Some of these women traveled with Jesus and the twelve full-time disciples from time to time, but particularly on his final trip to Jerusalem for the Passover Jesus was accompanied by *"many other women."* When Jesus was being crucified, Mark reports *"Mary Magdalene, Mary the mother of James the younger and of Joses, and Salome"* were present at Golgotha witnessing the agony of their Rabbi. John tells us Mary Magdalene and Mary the mother of Jesus stood close enough to the cross to hear Jesus. (See John 19:25-27.) Here we see the courage and devotion of these women who committed their lives to following Jesus.

John is the only one of the twelve male disciples reported to be present at Golgotha when Jesus was on the cross. (See John 19:25-27.) But two other men, both members of the Sanhedrin, also came forward to be counted with Jesus: Joseph of Arimathea and Nicodemus the Pharisee, members of the Sanhedrin. They believed in Jesus but had kept their faith secret to protect their political positions. Presumably neither was invited to the so-called trial by the Sanhedrin. But now that Jesus had been crucified, Joseph decided to break his silence and publicly identify with Jesus.

Jews scrupulously buried their dead before sundown on the day they died, and no burials were allowed on the Sabbath. (See Deuteronomy 21:22-23.) For that reason, Joseph appealed directly to Pontius Pilate for permission to remove Jesus' body and give him a quick burial. The ancient stone quarry where Golgotha was located, just outside the western city wall, had been converted into a garden cemetery with rock cut tombs in its walls. Joseph had recently constructed a family tomb in this very cemetery, so he stepped forward to bury Jesus in this tomb which had never been used before.

Jews buried their dead in rock cut tombs if they could afford it. These tombs were designed for extended families and could accommodate generations of burials. They either had carved-out shelves on which the body was laid or slots cut into the walls into which the body was slid. The outer entrance was closed by a stone plug, or in more expensive tombs was covered by a disk-shaped rolling stone set into a sloped channel that allowed the stone to roll across the low opening. After a body was anointed with scented oils and spices to mask the smell of decay, it was carefully placed in a linen shroud and wrapped from head to toe with strips of cloth and sealed in the tomb.

Joseph of Arimathea was captivated by Jesus' teaching and believed in him, but not enough to risk his political position. He wanted the benefits he perceived Jesus could offer without risking the loss of comfort, status, power, and wealth. But when he saw Jesus hanging dead on the cross, something broke inside of him. He knew he could no longer hide in the shadows, and so he *"boldly"* stepped into the light and counted himself with Jesus, who was now branded an outlaw. It couldn't have been good for Josephs' career, but his life was never going to be the same!

What are the ways in which you are avoiding being identified with Jesus because you are afraid it will have negative consequences? What step of faith could you take to become bolder and more courageous like Joseph and the women disciples of Jesus?

Reflect and Respond

What is Jesus saying to me right now?

What step of faith is Jesus calling me to take today?

DAY 63

READ AND LISTEN: MARK 16:1-8
Take a minute to listen for what the Spirit is saying in these verses...

COMMENT AND CONSIDER

Part of the rush to bury Jesus before sundown was because it marked the beginning of the Sabbath day. Jews consider sundown the end of one day and the beginning of the next. Therefore, Friday night is the beginning of the sacred day of rest on which no work is to be done, including burying the dead. The fact that Joseph and Nicodemus hurried to prepare Jesus' body convinced Mary Magdalene and some of the other women disciples that the men could not have done a proper job. They decided as soon as the Sabbath was over, they would go back to the tomb and honor their slain Rabbi by finishing the job of anointing his body.

Although the Sabbath technically ended on Saturday night, in the ancient world it was dangerous and considered morally questionable for women to go out at night. So just before dawn on the third day, Mary Magdalene led a group of at least five women disciples back out to that ancient rock quarry to visit the tomb of Joseph and anoint Jesus' body properly. On the way they began to realize it was going to be difficult to roll back that huge rolling stone. But when they arrived, to their great surprise, the stone had already been rolled up its track and wedged in place, opening the tomb!

When the women looked inside they saw a young man dressed in dazzling white. When they realized he was an angel they were afraid. He said to them, *"Don't be alarmed. You are looking for Jesus of Nazareth, who was crucified. He has risen! He is not here. See the place where they put him. But go, tell his disciples and Peter, 'He is going ahead of you to Galilee; you will see him there just as he told you.'"* Jesus, who was dead, is now gloriously alive! Not just spiritually, but physically. The angel pointed out that his body was no longer lying on the shelf in that tomb. The first declaration of the Good News of Easter was, *"He has risen!"*

When you visit Jerusalem today, the Church of the Holy Sepulcher inside the current walls of the city is said to mark the site of Jesus' death and resurrection. Although the maze of dark chapels and the layers of religious tradition can be disorienting, the archaeology and history all point to this as the actual location of that rocky outcropping in the quarry where Jesus was crucified and the actual tomb of Joseph of Arimathea from which Jesus was resurrected!

If Jesus rose from the dead, then everything he ever said is true. If Jesus rose from the dead, then he is able to keep all his promises. If Jesus rose from the dead, then he will raise us up as well. If Jesus rose from the dead, then death itself is defeated and God's Kingdom is forever! Jesus appeared to many different people in many different places at many different times. Most of the disciples died for their testimony that they saw Jesus die and then gloriously transformed and eternally alive. Some are willing to die for a lie if they are deceived and believe it to be true when it is not. But no sane person is willing to die for their testimony to the truth of something they know to be false.

It is not just a myth. It was not just the disciples' wishful thinking. It was not just an apparition they thought they saw. It is a real place. It is a real event. It was a real person. Jesus is really alive! How does the historical reliability of Jesus' resurrection affect your faith? What does it mean for you to walk more consistently in the victory Jesus has won over sin, death, hell, and the devil?

Reflect and Respond

What is Jesus saying to me right now?

What step of faith is Jesus calling me to take today?

DAY 64

READ AND LISTEN: MARK 16:9-20

Take a minute to listen for what the Spirit is saying in these verses…

COMMENT AND CONSIDER

These verses do not appear in the earliest manuscripts of the Gospel of Mark, which is why most modern translations put them in square brackets with explanatory notes. The earliest and most accurate copies end with verse 8: *They went out and ran from the tomb, because trembling and astonishment overwhelmed them. And they said nothing to anyone, since they were afraid.* Verses 9-20 appear in various later versions of this Gospel, seemingly because some people didn't like the way Mark ended his account of the Good News of Jesus. Of all the Gospels, Mark's is the only one that finishes with the women fleeing the angel in the empty tomb but not encountering the risen Jesus. When you have read the other Gospel accounts of the thrilling encounters the disciples had with the risen Jesus, it does seem an anti-climactic way to end the story, doesn't it?

This later ending seems to be a summary of the final chapters of Matthew's and Luke's Gospels that was added by ancient editors to fill in what was "missing" from Mark's account. But what if Mark ended his Gospel abruptly on purpose? What if he wanted to leave us hanging? Some novels and movies end their stories by neatly wrapping up all the details while the main characters ride off into the sunset or live happily ever after. Other stories end with unresolved plot lines and open-ended mysteries that leave the reader or watcher to wrestle with unanswered questions. This seems to be the way Mark chose to tell the story of Jesus. Kind of like Jesus' parables, he wants us to wrestle with the story until it changes us.

As the women run from the tomb in fear, where are they going? Do they understand what the angel told them? Will they really keep this incredible experience a secret? How can they keep from telling this story? What happens when the other disciples find the tomb empty? Will the angel appear to them as well? Is this a fulfillment of what Jesus promised would happen? How does Jesus' resurrection help us make sense of his horrible death? What did the angel mean when he said, *"He is going ahead of you to Galilee; you will see him there just as he told you."* When will we see him? Where will we see him? What will happen to us after we see him?

The original ending of Mark raises so many questions. This summary of the other Gospels' endings answers some of these questions, but it can be easy to read these verses without really asking the questions they answer. Maybe we need to wrestle with these questions first, so we put ourselves in the story. It wasn't just those women at the tomb who experienced all this. It wasn't just the male disciples hiding out in the upper room. It is our story too. We need to consider the meaning of the empty tomb. We need to meet the risen Jesus. We need to consider what his death and resurrection mean in our lives.

As we finish the Gospel of Mark, your story continues. What does it mean for you to believe Jesus is who he claimed to be, the anointed Son of God, the divine Son of Man, the I AM? What does it mean to be his disciple and live as part of his spiritual family? How can you participate in God's Kingdom every day? How can you share this Good News with those who need it so much? What does Jesus' death on the cross mean for you and for the whole world? How can the power of his resurrection flow through your life to do God's will on earth as it is done in heaven? Keep asking these questions as you follow Jesus one step of faith at a time…

REFLECT AND RESPOND
What is Jesus saying to me right now?

What step of faith is Jesus calling me to take today?

Footsteps Every Week: Review

Write a brief summary of what Jesus said to you each day this past week and the step of faith he called you to take:

Monday

Tuesday

Wednesday

Thursday

Friday

Saturday

Footsteps Every Week: Reflect

Big Picture
As you look over what Jesus has said to you this past week, do you see any themes? What is the most important thing you need to remember and believe?

Predictable Pattern
As you look over what Jesus called you to do this past week, is there a new predictable pattern he is inviting you to establish in your life with God and others?

Plant the Word
As you look over the readings from this past week, write out the passage that feels most important for you and memorize it over the next week:

MORE RESOURCES BY BOB ROGNLIEN TO HELP YOU FOLLOW JESUS

Find them all at www.bobrognlien.com

❖ **Books** | *Footsteps Every Day: Matthew, Luke, John*
- ➤ Continue the journey you have begun with daily Gospel readings and reflections on the Way of Jesus, illuminated by insights from history, archaeology, and culture. These three books of daily devotions together with the current volume can take you through all four Gospels in one year.

❖ **Book** | *Recovering the Way: How Ancient Discoveries Help Us Follow the Footsteps of Jesus*
- ➤ An in-depth treatment of Jesus' life illuminated by the history of his time, the cultural background of his world, and archaeological discoveries from our time. Includes over 100 photos, reconstruction drawings, and maps. Excellent for serious students and teachers who want to go deeper.

❖ **Book** | *The Most Extraordinary Life: Discovering the Real Jesus*
- ➤ A shorter telling of the true story of Jesus from his baptism to his resurrection, informed by history, archaeology, and culture. Each chapter begins with an expanded account of an event from Jesus' life which reads like a historical novel. Written for everyday people who know Jesus and those who want to get to know him for the first time.

❖ **Video** | **Recovering the Way: The Video Series**
- ➤ An in-depth video teaching series that illuminates the life of Jesus with thousands of full color photos, reconstruction drawings, and animated maps. The twelve 45-minute episodes

correspond to the twelve chapters in the book, *Recovering the Way* (see above) and will bring the Way of Jesus to life for you.

❖ **Trip | The Footsteps of Jesus Experience**
  ➢ A 14-day journey through Israel and Palestine, following the life of Jesus from birth to resurrection. We keep the group relatively small, stay in unique Christian guesthouses, drive ourselves in vans, do lots of walking off the beaten path, focus on the historically verifiable sites, and keep an intentionally spiritual focus. It is not a tour, but an intensive pilgrimage.

❖ **Podcast | The Footsteps Podcast with Bob Rognlien and Matt Switzer**
  ➢ In each episode Footsteps Experience leaders Bob and Matt take you on a journey to a significant site in the Holy Land and show how the discoveries there bring a specific biblical passage to life with new insights and applications.

❖ **Trip | The Footsteps of Paul Experience**
  ➢ A 15-day journey from Antioch to Corinth through Turkey and Greece, following the missional journeys of the Apostle Paul and his disciples. We keep the group relatively small, stay in boutique hotels with historical and cultural charm, drive ourselves in vans, go off the beaten path, focus on the historically verifiable sites, and keep an intentionally spiritual focus. It is not a tour, but an intensive pilgrimage.

❖ **Book | A Jesus-Shaped Life: Discipleship and Mission for Everyday People**
  ➢ A practical guide to putting the Way of Jesus into practice in your everyday life with the people who are closest to you. It tells the story of how Bob and Pam learned to pattern their lives and their family more intentionally after Jesus. It

also offers practical tools, vehicles, and strategies to make discipleship and mission a part of your daily life.

- ❖ **Book | Empowering Missional Disciples**
  - ➤ A resource for leaders who want to help those they lead to live a life that looks more like Jesus and produces more of the fruit he produced. Includes lots of field-tested tools and vehicles for multiplying missional disciples.

www.ingramcontent.com/pod-product-compliance
Lightning Source LLC
Chambersburg PA
CBHW070926010526
44110CB00056B/2162